NOT YOUR AVERAGE JOE

Cover, *A Light to the Gentiles,* ©Greg Olsen
By arrangement with Mill Pond Press, Inc. Venice, FL, 34285.
For information on art prints by Greg Olsen,
please contact Mill Pond Press at 1-800-535-0331.
Photo Images, Corbis
Wood Cut and Tool Illustrations, Jim Goold
Photography of St. Joseph statue, Mullins Studio
Cover and Graphic Design, Riz Marsella

ISBN 978-0-9743962-4-8
Library of Congress Control Number: 2004117252
Printed in the United States of America

RICK SARKISIAN, PH.D.

Not Your Average Joe

The Real St. Joseph and the Tools
for Real Manhood in the Home,
the Church and the World.

LifeWork
PRESS

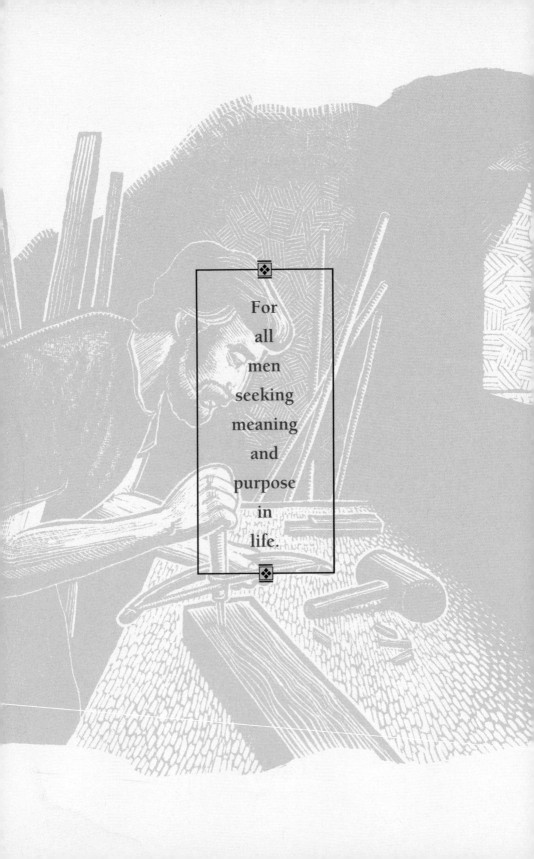

For
all
men
seeking
meaning
and
purpose
in
life.

ACKNOWLEDGEMENTS

This book would not exist without the inspiration and guidance of my cousin, Fr. Larry Toschi, OSJ. An expert on St. Joseph, Fr. Larry has many beautiful insights into this silent man, guided by the spirituality of his Order, the Oblates of St. Joseph.

The close collaboration of my long-time friend, Christopher Knuffke, was of huge value in developing many of the themes found in these pages.

From my earliest works, Mike Phillips has provided the highest level of penetrating editorial insights as well as input on chapter structure that became the template for what you are about to read.

The artistic talents of Jim Goold and Riz Marsella bring life to the text and the thoughts offered here.

Special thanks go to my patient, skilled secretary, Sandy Huerta, for what must have seemed like an endless series of transcriptions, revisions and rewrites.

As always, my wonderful wife and five children provide much in the way of support and real-life experiences that help me express what I want to say.

The influence of my dad, who died when I was 15, has always been part of my vocation as husband and father. I am also grateful for the love and support from my mom who is a close part of my life.

Finally, I must thank St. Joseph who has been such a big influence in my life. The words of St. Teresa of Avila and St. Joseph Marello contained on the next page promise real-world experiences for all of us.

Joseph is the last person who would want a book written about himself. I can only hope that this small effort brings the man closest to Christ the attention and devotion he deserves from us guys! ∎

"I wish I could persuade everyone to be devoted to this glorious Saint, for I know from long experience the benefits he obtains from God. I have never known anyone who is truly devoted to him and performs particular services in his honor, who did not advance greatly in virtue."

— St. Teresa of Avila

"St. Joseph remained ever calm, peaceful and tranquil, observing in everything a perfect conformity to God's wishes. St. Joseph desired nothing, wanted nothing that was not for the greater glory of God. He was thus almost imperturbable, even in adversities. Let us model ourselves after this sublime example and let us learn to remain peaceful and tranquil in all of life's circumstances."

— St. Joseph Marello

TABLE OF CONTENTS

FOREWORD

Today's Catholic and Protestant Christian men's movements are empowering men in their faith walk with the Lord. Undoubtedly, this is a move of the Holy Spirit for our day and age, because I believe our children are in worse danger than the infant boys during the time of Herod – the wicked tyrant that sent his soldiers to massacre all the boys of Bethlehem less than two years old. What an outrageous act of evil!

Fast forward to our age, where families are under a similar attack. Not a physical battle waged by a tyrannical king, but a spiritual battle launched by Satan himself. He covets the souls of everyone in our families, and uses time-tested tools like drugs, pornography and sexual temptation to drag many people down to hell. Our families are experiencing deadly assaults from advocates for abortion, homosexuality, stem cell research, cloning and euthanasia, creating a culture war that rages even within the walls of the Church.

Yes, Satan has an arsenal of formidable tools. And I know from my experience in boxing, karate and law enforcement that acquiring my own tools often kept me one step ahead of the enemy. Tools are essential for success in any battle. Unfortunately, I've noticed a real lack of tools (i.e. books, videos or other resources) that empower Catholic men to keep Satan at bay and live out their baptismal vows. Until now, that is. Because now we have a veritable "weapon of mass instruction" in this book by Dr. Rick Sarkisian.

Not Your Average Joe profiles the near perfect man – St. Joseph – a true "man's man" in every godly sense. This book is very practical, very biblical, very catechetical, very Catholic and very easy reading (a gift of Dr. Sarkisian's). The author weaves Josephite spirituality into great anecdotes from his personal experiences as a sacramentally married man and father of five.

This book is not written for the academic elite or scholarly types. Rather, it is written so that men from every walk of life can read it, understand it and apply it to their faith walk. In these pages you will discover an acute awareness of God's promises to fathers and their families.

Today's men must recover and reclaim the true teachings on fatherhood, and who better to help us than St. Joseph? Let us take St. Joseph as our powerful intercessor in heaven and our unfailing example on earth. Let us follow the Bible's command to "go to Joseph." It makes perfect sense: St. Joseph is, above all, the Protector of Families. He knows what it means to provide for a family, to protect them from harm. He knows the weariness that comes from working, providing food and establishing a home. He knows what it means to do whatever it takes to protect a family – even fleeing the country. No matter what your family wants or needs, you can be assured that St. Joseph – the ultimate "family man" – understands.

Indeed, go to St. Joseph. Use Scripture and prayer to guide you. And use this book as your travel companion. ■

Jesse Romero
Catholic Evangelist

INTRODUCTION

Not Your Average Joe.

Think that sounds a little too casual, a little too familiar, for a book about someone as universally loved and honored as St. Joseph? That certainly isn't my intention, since I have a great love for Joseph and have lived much of my life devoted to him. He's very real to me. But I've noticed a number of books, videos and works of art that elevate Joseph's holiness to the point where he becomes lofty and unapproachable, reigning aloof on his marble pedestal high above the fray of everyday life.

That's not the Joseph I know.

The Bible portrays Joseph as a rugged, hard-working man who was very much involved in the everyday life of his family and his world. To separate him from that world, to elevate him high above our trials and temptations, is to do a tremendous disservice to Joseph…and to ourselves. He has much to teach us about servanthood, integrity and authentic manhood. But we can only learn from him if we make Joseph part of our daily lives, and embrace the virtues that make him anything but "your average Joe." By doing so, we can become more than "average Joes" ourselves, demonstrating Joseph's virtues in the home, church, workplace and the world around us.

> He has **much to teach us about servanthood**, integrity and authentic manhood.

This book is about the vocation and mission of Joseph… who he was, and who we can become by living a life that parallels that of the man who

The name "Joseph" comes from the Hebrew expression "God (Yahweh) increases" or "God makes grow." (See Genesis 30:24 for Joseph's Old Testament namesake).

served Jesus like no other.

He also served Mary. As her husband, Joseph faithfully shared his life with the Blessed Virgin, the Mother of God. Often pictured standing on the moon, Mary reflects the light of her son. And with her, Joseph does the same. The triumph of Mary's Immaculate Heart and the conversion of sinners is inseparable from Joseph, who stands side-by-side with her.

Joseph is the silent one, the greatest Saint second only to Mary.

Joseph is a man of mystery. He was silent, obscure, hardly mentioned in Scripture. Yet he was chosen from among all men to protect the Holy Family and, with Mary, to raise the Son of God. He was husband, father, craftsman, protector and warrior against the powers of evil.

He was rugged and strong, yet gentle, kind, humble and ever-obedient to his God.

He had daily meals with Jesus. He taught Jesus the work of a craftsman. He read and discussed Scriptures with Jesus and was closer to Him than any other man. They traveled together, laughed together and worked together.

And Joseph will teach us how to travel with Jesus, laugh (and cry) with Jesus, and work with Jesus.

Joseph is the silent one, the greatest Saint second only to Mary. And we will find him in the silence of prayer,

leading us to Jesus in our heart, mind and soul. While silent in Scripture, Joseph is eager to speak to all men, single or married, about what it takes to be a real man.

What is a real man?

It is the man who puts God first, and allows his faith to filter into everything else.

It is the man who places great value on the virtue of humility, and embraces kindness, fairness and honesty in his relationships.

It is the man who values all human life – from the unborn to the elderly, from the physically handicapped to the able-bodied, from the developmentally-delayed to the mentally-gifted.

It is the man who prays and does so throughout the day, not just a few seconds before meals and bedtime. He has an ongoing awareness of God's presence as the hours stream past him each day.

And it is Joseph who will teach us how to become real men.

His workshop in Nazareth becomes our workshop now. His service to Christ reflects our fatherhood (spiritual or physical) now.

His tools are placed in our hands now. And each tool becomes an excellent metaphor for understanding Joseph's virtues as husband, father, craftsman and God's obedient servant. Joseph equips us with the skills we

chastity. If we lack confidence, he offers courage. If we lack parenting skills, he helps us. All in the name of his beloved son, Jesus.

In the pages that follow, you'll learn much about Joseph as a man called by God and sent to fulfill a particular mission in life. It's a mirror image of how God works in each of us... to be called and to be sent forth. You'll also be challenged to look at your life in fresh new ways, to see how you can change for the better by God's grace, and become a true reflection of Jesus in a world that needs to know Him.

You'll see why Joseph is so desperately needed to help us understand true masculinity, rather than the superficial version dished up by the world. Either we are seduced by the world's focus on pleasure, position, power and possessions, or we embrace God's design for authentic manhood.

Joseph will help us decide.

Now, more than ever, we need Joseph to stand shoulder-to-shoulder with us in the home, the workplace and the world at large. He loves to build... not just furniture, but lives. He will ask Jesus to give us the tools to do so and he will show us how to use them.

All of which makes St. Joseph far more than just "your average Joe." ■

need to be holy spouses, good fathers, diligent workers and faithful followers of Christ.

But he is much more than just a "tool guy." He is the protector of families, the role model for all men and the terror of evil spirits. He is a most powerful intercessor in God's heavenly realm and wants to assist us with our needs. If we lack purity, he offers

PART ONE

THE MAN

In our devotion to Joseph, it's sometimes easy to forget the fact that he was a real person – a flesh-and-blood craftsman from Nazareth, who experienced many of the same challenges and fears we all face in life. But we can learn much from the way he lived, worked and cared for his family.

Joseph was strong, yet gentle in spirit. A man of action, yet obedient to God's will. A working man, yet one who made time to be with his family and help Jesus grow in wisdom, knowledge and grace. None of Joseph's words are recorded in the Bible; in fact, his name is only mentioned a handful of times. Still, his actions in Scripture speak to us more clearly than recorded words ever could. And today from his workshop, he shows us how to use spiritual tools for becoming more and more like his son, Jesus. ∎

PATIENCE

Concrete is incredibly unforgiving. Once you mix it, pour it and let it harden, there's no undoing what you've done. Boy, did I learn that lesson!

I needed to create an 18-inch-deep foundation for a lamppost, which would be secured to it by 4 bolts set in concrete. After carefully digging the hole and pouring the concrete, I used the manufacturer's template to set the bolts in the wet concrete mix. The next day, I stood the lamppost upright and attempted to secure it to the foundation… only to learn that the bolts had shifted as the concrete had hardened. The bolt pattern no longer matched the holes in the lamppost, and I was forced to unearth a 150-pound chunk of concrete and start all over again. That required a whole lot of patience!

Isn't it good to know that God isn't like that hard, unforgiving concrete? He's always merciful and forgiving, patiently allowing us to repent and re-connect with Him despite our failings, sins and shortcomings. No digging required!

Patience requires self-control.

Patience is the virtue that allows us to quietly persevere in the face of troubles and provocation. Just think how patient Joseph was, enduring many trials and difficult times. He was willing to persevere through them all because he trusted in God and knew that day-by-day, he would see the Father's will unfold.

Patience requires self-control. Let's face it – there are certain things in life that drive us crazy and really test our patience. Whining children, a flat tire in the parking lot, a broken jar of jam on the kitchen floor, an overflowing toilet (which can be especially embarrassing when you cause it to happen at someone else's house). To stay under control, we often need to muster up as much self-restraint as possible, and that can seem nearly impossible.

Want an exercise in patience? Try going fishing with young children. If you've done this, you know exactly what I mean: tangled lines, snagged lures and hooks that seem destined to catch some part of your body instead of the fish they were meant for. I've even had one of my kids cast the line, rod and reel into the lake! Go fishing with youngsters, and you may not land any fish… but you'll definitely catch a lesson in self-restraint.

Did Joseph teach the Scriptures to Jesus? While "the Word made flesh" would have all knowledge in his divine intellect, mysteriously, he would need to learn it in his human nature. As His chosen father, Joseph would likely have taught Jesus to read the Scriptures.

Joseph wants to help us men – especially us dads…

Perhaps a better way for us to develop patience is to keep Joseph's example in mind and remember how he displayed great patience in poverty, persecution and other trying situations. That will gradually help us grow in this important virtue. It also helps to think of people we know that display patience, and try and emulate that aspect of their personality.

Joseph wants to help us men – especially us dads – grow in the virtue of patience so that we can demonstrate Christ-like qualities to our wives and children. We can accomplish this with the aid of Joseph's intercession and the regular, daily (even hourly!) practice of being calm, controlled and kind.

We never lack in daily opportunities for patience, whether we are at home, driving, working or shopping. I discovered this a few years ago when my wife was out of town on a ten-day trip, and I had sole responsibility for taking

our kids to and from school. One of those mornings, I was running late (as usual) and had to hustle the kids out the door, herd them into the car and race to school at full speed. I was a man on a mission, so single-minded in my purpose that it took my 9-year-old several attempts to get my attention. We were halfway to school before I tuned in to what he was trying to tell me: he had forgotten his shoes! At that point, I had only two choices: either explode in volcano-like eruptions of anger and frustration, or take a deep breath, turn the car around and quietly solve the problem. By God's grace I chose the second option, and not only learned a lesson in patience, but demonstrated it to my kids.

The case for patience is easily seen in the life of Joseph. The fruits of practicing the virtue of patience include less volatility in our relationships, less stress in our life, and a greater sense of enduring self-control. Let Joseph show you how to be more patient. Ask for his help in prayer. He won't let you down. ■

HUMILITY

A true car enthusiast never forgets his first restoration project. In my case, it was a 1929 Ford Special Coupe which I completely dismantled and rebuilt from the ground up. At one point, I was tightening the bolts around the transmission case, giving each one a heavy pull on the wrench to ensure maximum tightness. On the very last one, my enthusiasm got the best of me, and I ended up snapping the head clean off the bolt, leaving the threaded remnants buried inside the transmission case.

With a lot of sweat and scraped knuckles, I managed to extract the broken bolt shaft. But more importantly, I learned the value of realizing limitations…and staying within them.

It's easy for us, in our humanness, to exceed our limitations by relying on ourselves more than God. But He never "overtightens" us beyond our limitations; always offering us the grace to bear our trials. So instead of trusting in our own strength, let's humble ourselves before Jesus Christ and His grace for all our needs and for all good things.

> **It's easy for us, in our humanness, to exceed our limitations by relying on ourselves more than God.**

Joseph, with Mary, was given the amazing responsibility of raising the Son of God. He did so with the same humility that characterized everything he did. Joseph's humility is clearly seen in the way he surrendered himself to God's will: He didn't question God. He didn't need time to wrestle with it or "sleep on it." He just saw his place in God's plan of salvation and said "yes."

In his humility, Joseph showed great

power, strength and virtue. To achieve true manhood, all we need to do is look at Joseph's humble heart – the heart of a husband, a father… a servant of God. He knew that there was a particular role for him to play in the drama of salvation, and he consistently made choices that were in line with God's plan for him.

We can (and should) do the same. Are we willing to follow Jesus in such a way that we constantly seek his guidance? Are we willing to collaborate – to work with Jesus – so that God's plan for our lives can be implemented?

If we are, then we should seek Joseph's intercession to increase our humility and decrease our pride. Just as the presence of weeds hinders the growth of a fruit tree, the presence of pride defeats the growth of humility. We must examine ourselves to see the presence of pride in our lives.

Pride takes many forms: An inflated ego. Retained anger. Sarcasm. Pleasure-seeking. It is the most common and most fundamental vice, and one that must be challenged daily. Left unchecked, it can grow to dangerous – even disastrous – proportions.

When my grandmother arrived in the United States, she was barely 20 years old. She spoke only Armenian and knew little about American culture. One day, behind her small Central California farmhouse, my grandmother noticed that a small, green plant had sprung up from the soil. She began to water it daily, and the plant flourished, responding with vigorous growth. Soon it was two feet tall, then four feet, then a towering six feet tall. Finally, a neighbor broke the news to her: the plant she had been watering and nurturing was nothing more than a weed. Embarrassed by her naivete, she immediately cut it down.

Pride is a lot like that. The more we nourish our ego with "self," the more vigorous the growth of pride. The result? Pride eventually grows to greater and greater heights.

God has certainly come up with some imaginative ways to keep my ego in check! When I was first establishing my vocational rehabilitation practice, I thought I had it all: a Ph.D., a new suit and a fresh batch of business cards. I wanted to make a powerful impression on those who could refer their injury cases to me. One day, I ran into two of my most promising referral sources at a local retail store. I greeted them with all the poise and professionalism I could muster, doing my best to impress them while ignoring a rather persistent fly that kept buzzing around my face. Maybe God wanted to shut me up, or perhaps the fly was unusually inquisitive, but the next thing I knew, the little critter had flown right into my mouth!

Had the two men seen the fly go in? Should I pretend it didn't happen? Swallow? My mind was swarming with options as the fly frantically bounced from cheek to cheek in a desperate effort to escape. Finally, I 'fessed up, ejected the fly and sent it on its way, much to the amusement of the men I was speaking with. In fact, they "reminded" me of that incident for years afterward – a lesson in humility that kept on giving.

To become more humble like Joseph, we need to empty our egos, and become less of ourselves and more of Christ. Perhaps John the Baptist said it best when he spoke about the increase of Christ and the decrease of self (John 3:30).

Joseph was the first to give credit to God for all that happened in his life. This includes thanksgiving not just for the good, but also for the trials and sufferings. How difficult it must have been to depart abruptly for Egypt – a pagan land – not knowing how he would support and shelter his family. Yet within such trials we can find Jesus, who always loves to lighten our burdens.

Humility leads to trust. My son, Tommy, demonstrated incredible, childlike trust at the age of four, when he would routinely leap into our swimming pool and shout "Dad!" while in mid-air. He didn't know how to swim, but he knew I would hold him above the waterline. Are we willing to trust our Father in the same way?

Are we willing to draw attention away from ourselves and toward God as the source of all good things?

In 1999, I produced *Joseph: The Man Closest to Christ* – a video documentary that featured several Catholic speakers including evangelist Jesse Romero. A powerful speaker with a dynamic personality, Jesse had several memo-

rable segments – in fact, many people told me how much they enjoyed his part in the video! A year after releasing the video, I ran into Jesse at a conference and told him how much his comments had touched viewers. His reaction? "All the Glory to God." He drew no attention to himself. Instead, he immediately directed all the praise and positive feedback to our God. Now that's humility!

It's tough to be humble in a world focused on personal pride. We can see the rise of pride all around us, even in the evolution of magazine titles. Through the years, we've gone from *Life* to *People* to *Us* to *Self* – pretty revealing, eh?

Joseph will take us away from "self" and help us focus on Jesus and our relationships with others, seeing everything as a gift, to be used for the glory of God and the service of others. Go to Joseph in prayer and ask for his fatherly guidance and powerful intercession to grow in the virtue of humility. ∎

SIMPLICITY

I have been a collector since childhood. Stamps and base-ball cards at first. Then, as an adult, automobilia, Zorro and Davy Crockett collectibles, antique pedal cars and pre-war Fords. Through the years, I ultimately learned that the "hunt" is more fun than the "capture" – that seeking the hard-to-find is more exciting than actually owning it.

But there is another important lesson here that's easy to overlook in the pursuit of "things." A lesson about simplicity.

Joseph is a model of the simple life. He lived in poverty, yet he had the blessings of an "uncluttered" life. This allowed him to focus on what brings true meaning and purpose to life. He loved Jesus and Mary. He worked to support his family. He read and studied scripture. He had relationships with other believers.

He worshipped God.

It's within this kind of simple, ordinary, seemingly mundane life that we can discover daily opportunities for holiness. St. Joseph Marello, founder of the Oblates of St. Joseph, described "holiness in the ordinary" which is at the center of this religious order's spirituality. He said, "Be extraordinary in ordinary things."

> Joseph is a model of the simple life. He lived in poverty, yet he had the blessings of an "uncluttered" life.

The ordinary is all around us: doing housework, shopping for groceries, folding clothes, making dinner, driving to work or school. These are all opportunities for grace-filled moments and for listening to the quiet voice of God in our hearts.

In today's culture of activity and accumulation, we all have too much clutter, too many distractions. We allow ourselves to be overbooked, overcommitted and overrun with possessions. But Joseph lived a simple life free from the distractions that tempt us today. His focus was – and is – on the person of Jesus Christ. In the simplicity of his life, he found the profound. In the ordinary events of life in Nazareth, he found the mystery of God. In his poverty, he found rich treasure in Scripture and in devotion to Jesus and Mary.

Some years back, my wife and I built our "dream home" – a 4,000 square foot beauty located in an upscale neighborhood. During the year of design and the next year of building, I unwittingly placed greater and greater importance on the house. It was going to be the place where our children would be raised, and where their children would come to visit. It would be a place where memories were made and cherished for generations. From its features to its floorplan to its future, I had it all planned out.

God reminded me of what really matters: relationships.

For the first two years, the home lived up to my plans. Then one night as my wife and I returned home from an evening out, we noticed an eerie orange glow in the skies above our neighborhood. From our car windows, we saw that the usually empty streets were lined with cars, onlookers and camera crews from local television stations. Then I saw it – our dream home was engulfed in flames. And all my plans had gone – quite literally – up in smoke.

It was in that moment that God spoke to me. Not in a voice I could hear, but in the silence of my mind and heart. He reminded me that this house was really no more than a thing – a collection of sticks, bricks and nails – and that I had invested far too much in it.

God reminded me of what really matters: relationships. Those with my family, friends and the Church… with Jesus, Mary and Joseph. As sometimes happens in our spiritual journeys, it was a wake-up call. A call to simplicity.

So how can we eliminate the clutter and distractions from our lives so that we can enjoy the benefits of simplicity? Start small. Look around you right now. Do you see too many books and magazines? Give them away. Too many unnecessary possessions? Sell or donate them. If clutter isn't the problem, look at your lifestyle. Are you involved in too many hobbies, or spending too much time on recreation or entertainment? Cut back.

Try to take your life from "complex" to "manageable." Then go from "manageable" to "simple." Take small steps, and ask for Joseph to help you along the way. He's our model of simplicity, so he's got what it takes to get us where we need to be. In his poverty, he cared for the interests of Jesus. And he does the same today, bringing Jesus to those who are in need. Remember that needs extend beyond food, shelter and clothing. Even the wealthy and comfortable can be in spiritual or emotional poverty. Joseph brings the holiness of Christ to those who hunger and thirst, to those who have need for His true Presence.

> The **virtue of simplicity is** important **not only** in our lifestyle, but also in the practice of our **faith.**

The virtue of simplicity is important not only in our lifestyle, but also in the practice of our faith. I'm talking about a simple faith, one that sees Jesus Christ simply as Lord of all. This was powerfully illustrated when a group of Scouts was on a weekend campout. Sitting around the fire one night, the leader asked each Scout to say what they're thankful for. One by one, each offered thanks "for my parents," "for these beautiful mountains," "for friends." Then a Scout, blind since birth, took a turn and said, "I'm thankful for being blind." After a long silence, one of the other Scouts asked, "Why are you thankful for that?" The

blind Scout answered, "Because the first thing I'll ever see will be the face of my Lord Jesus in heaven."

Now that's a simple faith! Simple yet profound, saying more in one comment than a vast library of books could ever communicate about the subject.

Do you remember the simplicity of your childhood? I certainly do. Yo-yos, bicycles and baseballs. Comic books, western movies and black-and-white television. A little prayer book, a glow-in-the-dark rosary and a picture of the Holy Family. Simple joys that I still fondly remember all these years later.

It's these simple slices of life and faith that are well-remembered and well-used. They shape who we are, and forecast what we will become. If we latch on to the simple, the common, the ordinary that fills each day, then we follow in the footsteps of Joseph. Ask him to help you focus on the one thing necessary (Luke 10:42) and stay on course. ∎

Joseph probably lived a life typical of Nazareth's poor, subsisting mainly on fish from the nearby Sea of Galilee and living in a simple home of lime-stone and sun-baked bricks.

OBEDIENCE

I went on my first out-of-state trip when I was a young man of 18. My destination? The pretty little town of Amarillo, Texas. My purpose? Boot camp! I had just entered the California Air National Guard, and from my first moments in Amarillo I quickly learned the importance of following orders properly. Obedience became a survival skill – doing exactly what I was told, when I was told to do it. Not to anticipate commands, but to wait for the order and respond.

Joseph is one of the all-time great examples of obedience. He gradually came to know God's will, and responded with complete trust, surrender and compliance. For example, when he was told to leave immediately for Egypt, he went. He didn't weigh the options or discuss it with family and friends. He obeyed. He knew what God wanted and he conformed to God's will – a pattern that became a major part of his relationship with the Father.

Obeying always begins with listening to the Holy Spirit.

Can we be like Joseph in that regard? Yes, but it takes consistency. We need to pray daily for the grace to know God's will and respond with complete submission. To do any less is to remain distant from the true joy that occurs when we do what God wants.

Obeying always begins with listening to the Holy Spirit. How should we listen? In the same way Joseph did, by praying and reading Scripture and being ever-attentive to the voice of God in daily events and circumstances.

I once had what I considered a

world-class headache, the mother of all headaches – a pain so persistent, so oppressive that I went to the hospital to have it checked out. As it turned out, my headache was a symptom of something far more serious: viral meningitis – inflammation of the membrane that covers the brain. Isolated in a quarantine room for two days, I had plenty of time to think and pray. That's when my relationship with God came into clear focus. Locked away in a 10-by-10 foot room, lying in a 3-by-6 foot bed, removed from people, possessions and my position in life, I realized just how miniscule I was compared to the cosmos and God's eternal kingdom. And I saw that, ultimately, that's how we must face God – far removed from the world as we know it. Small, humbled and completely accountable for the level of obedience (or disobedience) we have displayed in our lives.

Joseph's life speaks volumes about faithful obedience. If we go to him in prayer and ask for his help, he will instruct us. He will show us how to listen to God and how to respond to what we hear. After all, Joseph's mission remains unchanged: he is called to help us discover the life-giving love of Jesus Christ and the eternal presence of the Father.

Obedience requires the heart of a child and a servant. Servanthood is not a bad thing, although to some it may sound as if serving someone (even God) takes away from our freedom. Actually, it's just the opposite. To serve God is an expression of our free will. We freely choose to be at the service of Christ and, in so doing, relish in the

joy of it all. There is no greater peace, nothing more fulfilling, than serving God through prayer, worship and our relationships with others.

SERVICE

Just as Joseph taught Jesus, we as fathers are called to teach obedience to our children. We have daily opportunities for doing this. And in the process of teaching them, they will learn what it means to conform to the Father's will. Whether we realize it or not, we dads are the first experience of God's paternity for our children. So, when we are kind, merciful, fair and forgiving, they remember that. And when we are angry, out-of-control, sarcastic or unforgiving, they remember that, too.

Like Joseph, we are accountable to God for our actions, especially in our home and family. So let us listen for the voice of the Good Shepherd and follow him. And teach our children to do the same. ∎

The Bible is clear about Mary's virginity. St. Thomas Aquinas was confident in Joseph's as well, "because we see nowhere that he had another wife, and because a saint does not succumb to fornication."

PRAYERFULNESS

I grew up building plastic models of just about every vehicle imaginable, from automobiles to amphibious tanks, airplanes to aircraft carriers. I especially enjoyed painting and detailing model cars, often adding "custom" touches like painted bolt heads and spark plug wires...even using fishing line to simulate fuel lines.

But my customization efforts paled in comparison to those of a young man I met a few years ago. He showed me an ingenious way of putting sound in model cars by using small headphone speakers as seat cushions. The wires from the speakers were then plugged into a music source and sound would boom out of an otherwise ordinary model car!

We're a lot like models ourselves, each of us needing assembly. God wants to help us with that process, and loves putting His personal touches on the details of our lives. And just as my young friend desired to install a sound system in a model car, God also desires that His voice be heard in our lives through Scripture and prayer. His "broadcast" then becomes an integrated part of who we are – a soundtrack for our spiritual journey.

> ## God also desires that His voice be heard in our lives through Scripture and prayer.

Joseph was tuned into that broadcast in a powerful way. He was deeply committed to prayer – a fact which is obvious in the way he discovered and followed God's will, and by the manner in which he conducted his life. He knew how to speak to God and, perhaps more importantly, how to listen to God.

There are times when the best way to "tune in" to God is through prayer without words. In the sanctuary of silence, we can experience the presence of God in our minds and hearts. Words can be distracting, but silence forces us to listen.

Of course, the world has its own broadcasts vying for our attention: news events, television and radio programs, work, school, recreation, leisure and home life. It's hard to listen to God and the world at the same time, just like trying to listen to AM and FM simultaneously. Praying effectively requires us to tune-out the world's broadcasts, so that we can hear the clear message of God and speak with Him in the silence of our hearts.

To grow in authentic manhood as modeled by Joseph is to pray regularly – daily – to our Lord. Go ahead and schedule a "prayer appointment" on your daily planner if it will help you set aside time for this. Or you may prefer to pray first thing in the morning or last thing each evening – whatever time you choose, do it consistently.

Can you imagine how beautiful it must have been to see and hear the Holy Family at prayer? The combined prayers of Jesus, Mary and Joseph must have been incredible! In stark contrast, I realized some years back that the only time my family prayed together was at dinner – grace – a total of seven seconds! Well, we changed that and now have evening prayers that include a rosary decade and special intentions.

Prayer keeps us on course as we make our earthly pilgrimage to the Father.

Prayer keeps us on course as we make our earthly pilgrimage to the Father. If you've ever been on a long international flight, you probably noticed that the airline provides an electronic world map on the plane's monitors, with a red line showing your progress between your points of departure and arrival. But what the monitors don't show are the many course corrections employed throughout your flight. Most commercial jets are actually "off course" much of the time, but don't be alarmed! The pilot constantly makes course corrections to keep the plane on its flight plan. We do the same thing on a smaller scale when we "nudge" the steering wheel while traveling down the road. If we fail to make adjustments and corrections while driving, we may end up off the road and, ultimately, in the hospital or cemetery.

Course corrections – made through a strong, consistent prayer life – are necessary for our spiritual journey as well. Just as conversation is the best way to get to know someone, prayer is

Why would Joseph, the "just man," consider divorcing Mary? Most likely because he believed he was unworthy to act as father to the Son of God rather than because he suspected unfaithfulness.

The relationship remained distant and cold. Then I learned why God had

> Just as **conversation is the best way** to get to know someone, **prayer is the best way** to get to know the **Father, Son** and **Holy Spirit.**

the best way to get to know the Father, Son and Holy Spirit. But it's important that we understand our part in the conversation. I learned that lesson some years back, when I was distressed about a less-than-satisfying relationship with a relative. I told God about the problem in prayer, and asked Him to bring harmony between my relative and myself, but nothing changed even after weeks of prayer.

allowed the problem to continue: in my prayers, I was not only giving God the problem, but also telling Him the solution! I had to recognize the importance of letting God come up with the solution, rather than treating Him like a vending machine. I learned to trust Him for the answer according to His will. And once I did that, peace was restored in my family relationship.

Where can we learn how to pray effectively? At Joseph's workbench. He knew how to converse with God and he had daily discussions with Jesus. In fact, no man spoke more with Jesus than Joseph. He'll show us how to develop a lifetime dialogue with the Son of God. ■

SILENCE

FAITHFULNESS

In 1989, a massive earthquake struck Armenia, the country where many of my ancestors lived. It was devastating. Over 30,000 people were killed in the blink of an eye. Within minutes of the quake, a father rushed to his son's school and his worst nightmare was confirmed: the building had been reduced to a pile of debris. The father had promised his son that he would always be there for him and, driven by this commitment, he began digging through the rubble. Other parents had given up any hope of finding their children alive, but the father kept digging. Brick by brick, stone by stone, he dug for the rest of the day and into the night. By morning, he still had not found his son, but undeterred, he kept digging with calloused hands and bleeding fingers all through the next day and night. Then, forty hours into his search, the father removed a boulder and heard something he feared he would never hear again: his son's voice! When he called the boy's name, he answered, "It's me, father! I told the others not to worry, that if you were alive, you would save us. I remembered your promise that you would always be there for me."

That's the kind of faith we see in the life of Joseph – a man who put his faith fully and completely in God. Nothing would interfere with his beliefs and commitment. In turn, God was faithful to Joseph, providing him the grace and blessings he needed to fulfill his vocation and mission.

Joseph will take us to new and deeper levels of faith – a profound faith – in which we will love God for who He is, rather than what He can do for us. As we are given the gift of faith, it becomes our responsibility to live it and share it with others – to let the light of truth reflect from us and illuminate the dark world around us.

On a missionary trip to China, an eye surgeon helped a man, nearly blind by cataracts, recover his eyesight. Weeks later, the doctor was surprised to find 40 other blind men seeking his help. They had walked over 250 miles through some of the most rugged and remote countryside in order to ask the doctor to restore their sight. When the doctor asked how they had made the difficult journey, the men explained that they had all held a rope that kept them togeth-er. At the front of the rope, leading the way, was the man who had his eyesight restored by the surgeon.

Joseph had an abiding certainty that God would provide for all the needs of his family – shelter, protection, clothing, food and work.

The man had been given the gift of sight, and he immediately wanted to share it. In the same way, when we are given the gift of faith, our desire should be to share it! To ensure that our faith remains strong and growing, we must nurture it through prayer, study, worship and in receiving the Sacraments of the Church.

Joseph had an abiding certainty that God would provide for all the needs of his family – shelter, protection, clothing, food and work. And with our trust placed in the One who created us, our needs will also be met. In fact, God knows much more about what we truly need than we do!

It is particularly within our struggles and brokenness that faith is so vitally important. I remember jogging one afternoon alongside my 7-year-old son, who was riding his bicycle. As we neared home, he raced ahead of me until he came to a fairly steep hill. It didn't take me long to catch up with him, as he was pedaling slower and slower, huffing and puffing with exertion and frustration. I placed my

Imagine the conflicting emotions Joseph must have felt upon hearing Simeon's prophecies – anguish at knowing a sword of sorrows would pierce Mary's heart, and joy for knowing his Son would be the source of salvation for the nations.

hand on his backside and helped him pedal to the top of the hill. That was years ago, but I have often thought of the beautiful metaphor there… how God comes to our aid during the uphill struggles we face.

Still, there are situations in life that seem utterly hopeless, in which God seems distant and our faith is tested. My father died just before my 16th

Still, there are situations in life that seem utterly hopeless, in which God seems distant and our faith is tested.

birthday. It was a time of deep doubt and confusion for me – after all, how could God let such a good man – a devoted husband and father – die? Even now, I still don't have all the answers. But I do know that God is real. He never left my father's side. He loved my dad completely, and loves me completely. That's what faith is all about: believing even when you don't fully understand.

Believe that Joseph's powerful intercession will transport your prayers, intentions and needs directly to the Sacred Heart of Jesus and the grace that flows from Him. ■

BELIEVE

HUMOR

It happened in a fancy French restaurant in downtown San Francisco. I had just been seated with two rehabilitation nurses who worked with me professionally on injury cases – three colleagues "dressed to the nines" and anticipating a pleasant get-together. As we waited to place our order, the nurse next to me buttered a slice of bread and began telling us a story about her daughter, using gestures that became more animated as the story went on. Suddenly, while punctuating the climax of her story, the piece of bread flew from her hand, shot across the table, hit the other nurse on her right cheek… and stuck there! (Yet another danger of using too much butter.)

Believe it or not, this situation isn't covered in the etiquette books. What was the "gentlemanly" thing to do? Reach across the table and peel the bread off her face? Offer her my napkin? Stick bread on my face? I was at a loss.

No doubt about it, humor is something we all need.

Fortunately, after a moment of awkward silence, we all enjoyed a hearty laugh. That moment couldn't have been more comically perfect if it had been planned and rehearsed. It was funny – truly funny.

No doubt about it, humor is something we all need. (Especially the upscale diners and snooty waiter who looked down their noses at us as we guffawed loudly.) I've often wondered: did Joseph have a sense of humor? We can only speculate, of course, but I would think he did. God would not have chosen a sour, grumpy old man to raise Jesus and be husband to Mary. I can easily see his amusement with Jesus, who, like most children, would laugh and have a joyful childhood. I can also envision Joseph laughing with his family and friends, looking at the human comedy that occurs in everyday living.

> I can **also envision** Joseph **laughing** with his family and friends, looking at the **human comedy** that occurs in everyday **living.**

Humor should be modeled in our own homes – not necessarily by creating an atmosphere of non-stop jokes and pratfalls, but in a way that encourages laughter without hurting someone else. Today's brand of popular humor is often rooted in sarcasm – cutting remarks meant to demean someone else. That kind of humor hurts, and has no place in the home – or the life – of a Christian.

Years ago, I was the featured speaker at the local chapter of a national service club. The fellow who introduced me to the audience thought he was being funny when he said, "As I bring Rick up to the podium, the words of John Wayne come to mind: the only good Armenian is a dead Armenian" (of course, John Wayne never said this). As someone of Armenian heritage, I found the "joke" to be in incredibly poor taste. Especially since 1.5 million Armenians were killed in massacres between 1915-1923. I

almost walked out, and looking back, I wish I had.

The point? We've got to be careful about our jokes and the subject matter. It shouldn't be too difficult, since there is so much "clean" material to laugh about in our daily lives. Material that brings about cheerfulness and joy.

Lighten Up.

Humor can also help us deal with situations that are annoying, frustrating or upsetting. Try laughing at them next time. After all, we do have a choice how we react – we can either lighten up or let things weigh us down. Let's choose to lighten up, and see if our problems are still as big as we think they are!

A classic example happened in my home several years ago. I was reaching

> God still loves us when we've goofed up. Our mistakes don't affect His love for us, or His care for our lives.

across the breakfast table with a full half-gallon of milk, attempting to pour it into a cup for one of my kids. The slippery carton dropped out of my hand, landed on its side and proceeded to cover the table in a flood of milk. The scene seemed to unfold in slow motion, as we were momentarily paralyzed by the hypnotic glug-glug-glug of escaping milk. By the time our brains had processed what had transpired, the carton was nearly empty. I could have reacted in anger or exploded in frustration, but by God's grace I saw the humor in the situation and we all shared a good laugh. (Not to mention a milkless breakfast.) To this day, "The Great Milk Spill By Dad" remains a treasured family story.

Need a good laugh? Look back on embarrassing moments in your life, and enjoy a laugh at your own expense. It always works for me! If you can laugh at yourself, you probably have pride under control…and that's good! God still loves us when we've goofed up. Our mistakes don't affect His love for us, or His care for our lives. Joseph can help us accept – and even laugh at – our imperfect world. It certainly wasn't a perfect world for him – far from it – yet he found a way to maintain a sense of fulfillment in his vocation and mission. ∎

Think about it: Joseph must have possessed an incredible level of faith and love in order to live side-by-side with two people exempt from original sin!

LAUGHTER

PART TWO

THE CALL

G od has a purpose for each of us — a vocation to be
lived out in faith and obedience to help us find fulfillment in this life and in eternal life. God calls some to
the priesthood or religious life. Others He calls to live as vowed
singles for Christ and His Church. And many are called to
marriage and raising families. God hand-picked Joseph and
lovingly prepared him for a very special vocation: becoming the
husband of Mary and the chosen father of Jesus. In living out
his vocation, Joseph was obedient in silence and simplicity.
A man of prayer. A faithful husband. A loving father. A friend
who helped other men. A man after God's own heart. ∎

VOCATION

I was single for a long time. In fact, I was nearly 32 years old when I got married. I knew throughout most of my adult life that God was calling me to the vocation of marriage, although I did explore the priesthood for a short time. I didn't realize it until I married my wife, but now I know the call to marriage is a "vocation within a vocation" – that within the context of seeking a marriage partner, I was also being called to marry a particular woman. Thanks be to God, I found her! But our marriage vows were only the beginning of the new life that awaited us. That's why graduation ceremonies are called "commencement exercises" – marriage, like graduation, is a beginning, not an ending.

When Joseph began to see the divine plan God was laying out for him, he responded by fully accepting his personal vocation. He was able to accept a life of virginity, taking Mary into his house and caring for her and Jesus. Joseph and Mary were fully committed to accepting God's will, uniting with Heaven at the birth of Jesus, and becoming an "earthly trinity" that reflected the Holy Trinity in Heaven. Joseph teaches us that vocation is about call (God's) and response (ours).

> Joseph **teaches us** that **vocation** is about **call (God's)** and **response (ours).**

Our vocation involves the universal call in baptism to seek holiness, and the specific call to a state of life (like marriage, the priesthood, religious and single life). Pope John Paul II writes, "The fundamental objective of the formation of the lay faithful is an ever-clearer discovery of one's vocation and the ever-greater willingness to live it so as to fulfill one's mission." (John Paul II, *Christifideles Laici #58*)

> He's alive in the **hearts**, minds and **souls** of these little ones and wants to use **parenthood as a means** for them to know that He **is present,** revealing Himself in the Liturgy – in **His Word** and in His **Sacraments.**

about God's will with trust and confidence that the One who made them will be faithful in providing answers. They'll know what God wants because He is real, not just a "force" or "concept." He's alive in the hearts, minds and souls of these little ones and wants to use parenthood as a means for them to know that He is present, revealing Himself in the Liturgy – in His Word and in His Sacraments.

To discover our vocation is to cooperate with Christ who says, "Follow me." He holds the only true map for our lives. But some of us grapple with a more basic decision: is life a personal vocation or a personal project? If you believe that God created you and has a unique plan for your life (both are true, by the way!), then seek His will with all your heart, because it's the only way to live a life of purpose, meaning and happiness. If you think your life is a "do-it-yourself project," then you're on your own! You've decided to build a house without a blueprint.

Joseph's life is one of the best vocation stories of all time. Why? Because he lived a life of docility, surrendering his will to God's. He didn't question the plans God laid out for him, he just accepted them and followed them faithfully.

If you're a father, I want to encourage you to present the subject of vocations to your children as early in their lives as possible. Even 5-year-olds can begin to develop an awareness that God will call them to a particular state of life. They can be encouraged to pray

Joseph is considered the "patron of workers" not because he worked more than other saints, but because his work had a special purpose: to raise and educate the Son of God and support the Holy Family. From Joseph, Jesus learned and practiced his trade until he began His public ministry.

I'll never forget meeting Dr. Alan Keyes, former U.S. Ambassador and presidential candidate, broadcast commentator and the most articulate defender of unborn children that I have ever heard. Keyes is a true moral conservative and a riveting public speaker, and I must admit to being a bit nervous about meeting him. He was the first person I interviewed for my video documentary, *LifeWork: Finding God's Purpose for Your Life*.

As it turned out, my nervousness was unfounded. Keyes was friendly and genial, and offered many wonderful insights during the interview. In particular, he told me that everybody in society is encouraged to ask the wrong questions such as, "What do I want?" "What fulfills me?" and "How will I be satisfied?" These questions define happiness as if it's all about our selfish satisfaction. Keyes said it is a tremendous breakthrough when we finally reach the point where we've stopped asking what we want and start asking what God wants.

> We get **so wrapped up** in our wants, **our needs, our passions,** that we can't see they don't lead to **true peace.**

Yes, Dr. Keyes, you hit the bullseye! We get so wrapped up in our wants, our needs, our passions, that we can't see they don't lead to true peace. The pleasure and happiness we derive from worldly pursuits are incredibly short-lived. But when we follow Joseph's example, we discover something even higher than happiness: joy. And joy endures eternally.

Let Joseph take you to Jesus and you'll find joy, guaranteed. ∎

DIVINE PLAN

Joseph's mission continues today. Just as he cared and provided for Jesus and Mary, always trusting in God's providence, Joseph will care for us and will encourage us to trust in God.

STRENGTH

It was a dark and stormy night (sounds like the opening line of a bad novel, doesn't it?). I was traveling across the San Mateo Bridge to visit my brother in the San Francisco Bay area. The storm was intense – pounding rain, howling winds, almost zero visibility – and the traffic was heavy.

The narrow bridge is little more than a stretch of roadway running barely above the water of the bay, and that night the dark, churning ocean waves seemed to be grasping for my car, ready to pull me off the bridge and drag me down into the icy depths below. I have to admit, I was frightened. I prayed fervently, and I knew I had to "brave it out" – after all, with so much traffic around me, what choice did I have but to continue moving forward? After a few miles, the roadway rose to a higher bridge span, and the ocean's threat steadily diminished until finally I was driving on solid ground.

We are each called upon to be brave in different ways and at different times. And Joseph has a lot to teach us about bravery, strength and toughness.

> And **Joseph has a lot to teach us** about bravery, **strength** and toughness.

He was strong in the face of adversity and the poverty of his time – a strength he found in God's mantle of grace that covered his family. He was also rugged and physically strong. He had to be in his line of work. While most of us think of Joseph as a carpenter, the Greek word for his craft is "tekton" – a "worker of hard materials." So it's likely that Joseph worked with heavy wood, stone… even metal. And he was also strong in the "stalwart" sense of the word, standing up to whatever might threaten or harm his family.

In the 1930s, my dad was a big rig

truck driver – a demanding job for a young man, but one he handled with great skill. His greatest challenge came one afternoon on California's notorious "Ridge Route" – a steep, harrowing descent from a high mountain range into the valley below. The Ridge Route tested the mettle of every driver, but particularly big rig drivers whose tons of cargo propelled them down the grade with frightening momentum. My dad had just begun his descent when he came to the sudden, sickening realization that he had lost his brakes. He and his 70,000 pounds of rolling freight were out of control.

As news of dad's runaway truck spread, police units were called to act as safety escorts, but they couldn't keep up. Terrified motorists cleared a path for dad's truck, which careened crazily around curves and gained deadly momentum on the straight-aways. By God's grace, my dad was able to stay on the road as the Ridge Route gradually leveled off into the valley floor, and the truck eventually rolled to a safe stop. Exhausted from the sheer stress of his ordeal, my dad passed out. But he survived, thanks to his strength – not just his physical strength, but more importantly, the strength of his resolve as he fully devoted his energies to keeping himself and others from tremendous potential harm.

> As **Protector** of the Church and Terror of Evil Spirits, he is **committed to guard** and defend us from **spiritual injury.**

That's the kind of resolve that Joseph has for us. As Protector of the Church and Terror of Evil Spirits, he is committed to guard and defend us from spiritual injury. He brings fortitude to situations that trouble or endanger us, whether it's spiritual attack, physical harm, illness, temptation, difficult relationships or habitual sin. Through his virtues of strength and fortitude, Joseph's "staying power" can get us through whatever difficulties we face. He helps us grow even stronger in these key virtues.

That's pictured powerfully in the Chinese bamboo tree, which only appears to grow an inch or two during its first four years. But in its fifth year, the bamboo shoots up to heights of 60 feet or more. What's going on in those

SACRAMENTS

first four years? The bamboo is growing like crazy, but not above ground where it can be seen. In fact, its roots are spreading far and deep into the earth, providing a strong anchor for the height that will follow. Similarly, we need to be firmly rooted in Christ so that we are well-anchored when the world tries to pull us down or the storms of life threaten to blow us over. Joseph shows us the way to Jesus and asks for His divine grace to feed the soil in which we are rooted. We can

Surviving life's storms
sometimes requires
supernatural strength.

also nourish that soil with daily prayer, the Word of God and the Sacraments.

Surviving life's storms sometimes requires supernatural strength. This was brought home to me in the summer of 1969, when I was stationed in Gulfport, Mississippi for training with my California Air National Guard unit. Little did we know that within days of

Joseph was more than a carpenter. He was a craftsman described by the Greek word "tekton" - a worker of "hard materials" like wood, iron and stone.

FITNESS

our arrival, we would be tested not by an enemy or military action, but by the primitive power and unleashed fury of Hurricane Camille.

Camille struck in the dead of night while we took shelter in barracks made of concrete block and wood. The screeching wind ripped the roof right off our building, exposing us to torrents of rain from the skies above and a parade of snakes seeking higher ground from the swamps below. Many of us sandwiched ourselves between mattresses for protection from flying debris. While I'd like to tell you I was calm in the face of danger, I'd be lying – I was terrified! But God gave me the inner strength and fortitude to ride the storm out. When it was all over, our camp looked like a war zone after heavy shelling. Thanks be to God, we were all safe and accounted for, but 256 others in Mississippi and Louisiana lost their lives to Hurricane Camille.

Strength is a curious human quality. It involves more than mere muscle power, and includes the mind and spirit as well. To grow stronger in any of these areas, we need to combine exercise and nutrition.

After being a runner for over 25 years, I decided to add weight lifting to my weekly exercise regime. I thought I was in shape, but boy was I wrong! While my cardiopulmonary system was fit from running, I had grossly neglected muscle maintenance and so began the tedious process of strength training and making drastic changes in my diet. I learned from a trainer that if I wanted to improve my muscle tone or size, I had to support my exercise program with the right combination of protein, fat and carbohydrates.

> ## As men of faith, it's important that we remain strong in body, mind and spirit.

The same holds true for our mind and spirit where, through prayer, sacraments and reading Scripture, we strengthen ourselves in these areas… as Joseph did. That's the kind of exercise/nutrition program that delivers a big spiritual payoff… the ultimate "diet" plan.

As men of faith, it's important that we remain strong in body, mind

and spirit. That's because we are "counter-cultural," going against the grain of worldly culture that promises short-lived pleasure rather than long-lasting joy.

God calls us to be brave, even fearless! Like Joseph, we must not yield to the pressure of the secular world that surrounds us. Our dedication is to the person of Jesus Christ. And Joseph, as our "personal trainer," will give us the courage to abide in Him. ∎

Joseph shows us that real manhood nothing to do with wealth or machismo. It is based on the kind of strength that comes from faith and a close relationship with Jesus.

FORTITUDE

KINDNESS

Fred Rogers was best known to generations of TV as the beloved host of "Mr. Rogers' Neighborhood." I think what appealed to adults and children alike was his pleasant nature – he always appeared to be kind, thoughtful and full of good will. Many who knew him have said there was no difference between his on-camera persona and his off-camera persona. He was consistently kind, whether or not the camera was rolling.

While intended for children, "Mr. Rogers' Neighborhood" was among my favorite shows to watch after a tough day at work. How could I stay upset when Mr. Rogers posed thought-provoking questions like, "Do puppies sleep in pup-tents?" He was a one-of-a-kind fellow – calm, kind and cooperative with others.

But Fred Rogers didn't have a corner on the kindness market. In a profound way, Mother Teresa of Calcutta personified kindness in her work with "the poorest of the poor." Along with her Religious Congregation, she unceasingly assisted the forgotten, sick and dying in the name of Christ's love and the extension of His kindness.

> Being **consistently kind** means overcoming our **self-centeredness.**

Similarly, Joseph's unselfish life was marked by thoughtfulness, understanding and good deeds. He must have been an image of kindness in the way he interacted with those in the village around him. Of course, he unfailingly remained generous and kind with Mary and Jesus as a devoted husband and father.

Being consistently kind means overcoming our self-centeredness. Ask yourself: if you died today, would people remember you as a kind person? Would they talk about your kindness at your funeral? Could they give examples of your acts of kindness? (Can you?)

> **In situations** where we can't directly **intervene with kindness,** we can do so indirectly through **prayer and charitable contributions.**

If you need to grow in this virtue, look for examples of kindness in others. I've found a great example in my son, Andrew. He has been a faithful friend to one of his fellow fifth-graders – a boy who was born without the lower portions of his legs. Andrew has fully accepted the boy's limitations and doesn't treat him as someone fragile or impaired. Through his kindness, Andrew's attitude takes the "dis" out of "disability," placing value on what his friend can do rather than what he can't

do. (Wearing prosthetic legs, the young lad is able to play basketball and flag football!)

How often do we adults fail to accept someone because of their flaws and failings? Many turn quickly away from the imperfections of humanity; they have no time for tolerance, goodwill or positive regard. As Andrew accepts his little friend, so Jesus accepts us with all of our flaws. We are called to be the image of Christ to others, reflecting His compassion, concern and kindness to all God's creatures.

Think of someone right now that tries your kindness. Don't settle for someone "easy," but think of someone to whom it would seem impossible to be kind. Now make a diligent effort to be kind to that person for seven days. Make him or her your "project" for the coming week. You might want to follow the philosophy of the Boy Scout slogan: "Do a Good Turn Daily," looking actively for opportunities to spontaneously help others in need with the hand of kindness. I think you'll find that showing kindness gets easier the more you do it, just like exercise or weight training.

In situations where we can't directly intervene with kindness, we can do so indirectly through prayer and charitable contributions. Every time we pray for another, it's kindness. Giving money to a relief organization is kindness. Donating clothing and household items to a charity is kindness. So look for different ways to express kindness in the world around you.

In your devotion to St. Joseph, consider the unselfish and thoughtful life he lived. What a great model for all men – husbands, priests, religious brothers and lay singles – showing us how to be tolerant with other people, understanding when there is a change of plans and thoughtful in recognizing the needs of others.

Kindness: genuine, generously given and gentle in nature.

Lastly, let your kindness be genuine, not phony – consistent, not just convenient. A friend told me about a homeless fellow who approached him as he was having lunch outdoors. The man asked for some milk to settle his stomach. My friend promptly gave him a dollar, but later realized that he did so only to be rid of him. He didn't want his lunch interrupted. The genuinely kind (and Christ-like) response would have been to buy the man some milk and stay with him as he drank it.

Kindness: genuine, generously given and gentle in nature. That's what we find in abundance in the life of Joseph. ■

Why do some say Joseph and Mary had other children? They are likely misunderstanding or misinterpreting biblical references to Jesus' "brothers" – a word which, in Aramaic, carries the much broader meaning of "relatives."

TOLERANCE

MANHOOD

I attended the University of California at Berkeley (aka "Berserkly"). Near the campus was the Center for Independent Living, a facility that helped the most severely disabled gain increased independence for living on their own. It was common to see people from the Center on or near the campus. As I walked to class one morning from my apartment, I saw two young men coming toward me, one in a wheelchair and the other pushing him. As we passed each other, I noticed that the fellow in the wheelchair was a quadriplegic, paralyzed from the neck down. The man pushing him was blind.

What a powerful image of how men need to help each other on their journey of faith. Proverbs 27:17 tells us that one man "sharpens" another just as iron sharpens iron. One of the men who keeps me "sharp" is my cousin, Father Larry Toschi, OSJ. I never really knew him in childhood, but after getting to know him as an adult, I learned that he is a priest in the Oblates of St. Joseph. As my friendship with Father Larry has grown, so has my desire to know St. Joseph – to understand his silence in Scripture, his role in the salvation story and his patronage for these times.

> There is **no better example of authentic manhood,** apart from **Jesus, than his chosen father, Joseph.**

In the introduction to this book, I expressed some of my thinking about what it takes to be a real man. There is no better example of authentic manhood, apart from Jesus, than his chosen father, Joseph. That's why this book is centered on him, to help us embrace those qualities in Joseph that we need in order to develop into the men God wants us to be. A devotion to Joseph will result in at least two benefits (and probably many more): we will draw closer to our Lord and Savior Jesus Christ and we will acquire more and more Joseph-like qualities and virtues for our journey of faith.

Understanding authentic manhood is important not just for ourselves, but also for our sons and daughters. We've got to teach them the qualities of being a real man…because if we don't, the world will. Do we want to give our children the image of a godly man of faith, or a man who clings to the world's superficial portrait of masculinity? We've got to choose. And when we choose authentic manhood, we've got to share it with both our sons and our daughters, letting them see what it takes to be a real man in the eyes of God. Our kids are only young and impressionable for a short time; so we must consider this the opportunity of a lifetime.

Bill Havens had a lifetime opportunity when he was chosen to represent the United States in a canoe racing event in the 1924 Summer Olympics in Paris. His wife was expected to deliver their first child during the games, and Bill had to make a decision: either participate in the event and miss the birth of his first child, or withdraw from the competition and be there with his wife during the delivery. He chose to remain behind, and on August 1, 1924 – four days after the competition – his son, Frank, was born.

A heartwarming story, to be sure, but that's not the end of it. During the 1952 Summer Olympics in Helsinki, Bill Havens received this telegram:

> **Dear Dad, Thanks for waiting around for me to get born in 1924. I'm coming home with the gold medal you should have won.**
> **Your loving son, Frank**

Bill Havens traded what most considered the opportunity of a lifetime for the real opportunity of a lifetime. And left us with a powerful illustration of real manhood.

We have amazing opportunities before us in the way we raise our children. And Joseph is standing by, ready for us to enlist his help in taking advantage of those opportunities. Let Joseph teach us what it takes to be true men of faith, committed to Jesus Christ, His Word and His Church. ■

FATHERHOOD

I grew up in the 1950s and '60s, when America's small screens were filled with larger-than-life heroes like Superman, Daniel Boone, Davy Crockett and many others. But no character – real or imagined – could top my favorite hero: Zorro. Outfitted with his black mask, flowing cape and trusty sword, Zorro was the coolest of the cool, dashing in to save the day, week after week on our television.

My dad, who could make just about anything, made me a fabulous sword just like Zorro's as part of my Halloween costume one year. He crafted the "blade" from a length of copper tubing, the handle from wood wrapped in black electrical tape, and the handle guard from a piece of aluminum. He even made me a scabbard that hung from my belt! That Halloween, I was the envy of the neighborhood.

My dad helped me conform to the image of my hero, Zorro. And today, I see how Joseph helps us conform to the image of Jesus who is the image of our Heavenly Father. This occurs through divine grace, which literally transforms our lives and helps us be like Jesus to others.

Fatherhood also extends to the **vocation** of the priesthood, diaconate and **consecrated** religious life.

Our fatherhood, like Joseph's fatherhood, is an image of our Heavenly Father. That's a lot of responsibility, but indeed, we men must reflect the kindness, fairness and forgiveness of our Father in Heaven to our children. And Joseph is ready to show dads how to do their job – how to use the tools given them by God to raise their children properly and to be holy spouses.

Fatherhood also extends to the

vocation of the priesthood, diaconate and consecrated religious life. Their call is to a spiritual fatherhood over those in their parish or community. But regardless of the type of fatherhood to which we are called, we can entrust ourselves to Joseph, just as Jesus and Mary put themselves entirely into his care.

Driving along the freeway one morning, I was thinking about some news that my wife had just given me: she was pregnant with our fifth child. I began to "do the math" and realized that I would be 48 at her birth, 65 when she finished high school and well over 70 when she finished college. None of those numbers put a smile on my face, and God showed me why – I was thinking about myself rather than the precious gift He had given us! I was ashamed, and knew that I should be humbled before God knowing that in His mysterious ways, He felt my wife and I were actually worthy to raise another of His souls. There was an immediate shift in my thinking, and I became thankful and at peace with God's providence. I put away my mental calculator and started smiling.

WHAT CAN YOU AS A CHRISTIAN MAN DO TO BETTER LIVE OUT GOD'S MODEL OF FATHERHOOD?

HERE ARE SOME PRACTICAL STEPS YOU CAN TAKE:

1 MAINTAIN A GENTLE SPIRIT. REFLECT GOD'S MERCY AND FORGIVENESS WHEN CORRECTING YOUR CHILDREN'S BEHAVIOR.

2 SPEND AS MUCH TIME AS POSSIBLE WITH YOUR CHILDREN. READ TO THEM, EAT WITH THEM, PRAY WITH THEM, PLAY WITH THEM.

3 TEACH VIRTUES BY EXAMPLE. ACTIONS DO SPEAK LOUDER THAN WORDS.

4 BE A DAILY EXAMPLE OF PRAYER, HONOR AND INTEGRITY. BE REAL ABOUT IT.

5 SHOW AFFECTION DAILY TO YOUR WIFE AND CHILDREN. LET YOUR CHILDREN LEARN ABOUT LOVE THROUGH YOUR EXAMPLE.

6 TAKE CONTROL OF YOUR HOME. ESTABLISH FAIR RULES. DON'T ALLOW WHAT YOU DON'T APPROVE OF.

7 LOOK FOR KEY MOMENTS TO DEFINE TRUE JOSEPH-LIKE MANHOOD TO YOUR SONS (AND DAUGHTERS). LOOK FOR WAYS TO TEACH THEM PERSONAL AND SOCIAL SKILLS.

8 MAINTAIN SELF-CONTROL. WHEN YOU ARE ANNOYED, FRUSTRATED, ANGRY OR OUT-OF-CONTROL, YOU NO LONGER REFLECT THE IMAGE OF GOD THE FATHER.

9 PROVIDE COACHING IN THE DISCOVERY OF LIFE-PURPOSE. HELP WITH CAREER CHOICES AND EDUCATIONAL OPTIONS.

10 TELL YOUR CHILDREN ABOUT MEN YOU KNOW WHO DEMONSTRATE THE QUALITIES OF AUTHENTIC MANHOOD AS REFLECTED BY JOSEPH.

Even though Joseph is "silent" in Scripture, his sanctity speaks much more clearly than any words that could have described it.

Let us **never forget to give thanks** to God in all things.

Let us never forget to give thanks to God in all things. When I was an infant, my father came down with what was then a life-threatening disease: coccidioidomycosis, or "Valley Fever." He nearly died but, by the grace of God and extensive medical treatment, he survived. In thanks to God, my father converted from the Armenian Orthodox Church to the Roman Catholic Church and lived a devout sacramental life for the remainder of his years. I have always remembered that example of gratitude. May all men unite in giving thanks to God for the gift of Joseph's fatherhood and his paternal guidance to the Father's Son, Jesus Christ. ■

HEAVENLY FATHER

PURITY

I was at the checkout counter of a large retail chain store with one of my sons, then age 14. As usual, a rack of tabloid magazines was prominently on display. But this particular display was unusually offensive, graphic in both word and picture. I'm not talking about idle Hollywood gossip or aliens abducting Elvis, but content that was extraordinarily perverse and explicit. I immediately called for the manager, who listened as I registered my objections. I explained that I was trying to foster an environment for my family that was free from moral assaults. I knew my children would eventually be exposed to such a culture, but I didn't expect it to happen at the checkout of a supposedly "family-friendly" national retailer. To my surprise, the manager not only agreed with my concerns, but removed all copies of the tabloid in question! A small battle was won, but the war wages on. By the following week, more offensive tabloids were on display.

> In the **Beatitudes** (Matthew 5), **Jesus** tells us that the pure of **heart** are blessed for they shall **see** God.

The virtue of purity carries with it the requirement of modesty in our thoughts, words, behavior and dress. If we remain pure, like Joseph, we will be free from moral fault. We will be innocent – a concept that ought to be treasured, yet is ridiculed by the secular world around us. Another type of modesty maintains a moderate (not inflated) image of ourselves – men who know their limitations.

With God's grace, we will prevail in

the battle for purity. Make no mistake, it won't be easy. Every day, we are faced with a steady onslaught of flesh, sexual innuendo and all forms of immorality. Remaining pure is a huge challenge, as we attempt to "swim" through the sewage dumped on us daily from titillating television programs, slick magazines and the seemingly bottomless cesspool of pornographic websites. We must pray for the strength to control our thoughts and desires.

We must never let our guard down. **Temptation** to sins of the flesh **swarm around us like flies** at a summer barbecue.

Thoughts lead to desires.
Desires lead to actions.
Actions lead to habits.
Habits shape our character.
Character determines our destiny.
And it all begins in the mind.

(Based on a talk given by
Fr. John Hardon, S.J.)

In the Beatitudes (Matthew 5), Jesus tells us that the pure of heart are blessed for they shall see God. This is our real yearning. All the beauty and pleasure of this created world cannot satisfy our desire to see the Creator Himself. Impurity clouds this vision and can eternally rob us of it. Mastering our thoughts is one of the most difficult challenges in our human nature.

The Church teaches that chastity is one's ability to uphold the integrity of the powers of life and love placed on him. Chastity is a virtue to be lived according to our state of life. So the married person must remain as chaste as the celibate priest. Regardless of our state in life, we can look to Joseph to show us how to be chaste.

We must never let our guard down. Temptation to sins of the flesh swarm

around us like flies at a summer barbecue. Self-mastery is an apprenticeship that never ends. As one elderly priest told me, "Temptation doesn't stop until 30 minutes or so after you die."

Fathers should look to Joseph for guidance in practicing the virtues of purity, modesty and chastity. We need his fatherly guidance in the proper ways to raise our children and keep them morally straight. I have had talks and on-site "field trips" with my kids on the subject of bad magazines, bad

CDs, bad movies and bad language. I've told them the bad words they are sure to hear and what these words mean. Let me tell you, it wasn't easy doing this with them in their innocence and youth. But parents must equip their children with the skills and tools they need to face adulthood with the confidence, integrity and high moral values championed by St. Joseph, model of purity. We can teach this through the use of Scripture, the Rosary, daily prayer, and frequent confession and Holy Communion. It's strong medicine, but then again, we're fighting a powerful disease. ∎

Which virtues best describe Joseph? Among many fitting virtues, the most obvious are faith and hope (as he trusted in God's providence), obedience (as he followed God's plan), humility (as he served his family) and chastity (as he lived a virginal marriage).

MODESTY

COMMITMENT

We are surrounded by committed people. Athletes committed to their sport. Soldiers committed to their mission. Singers committed to their music. Teachers committed to their students. Doctors committed to their patients.

But I was particularly struck by the commitment made by some one hundred men about to be ordained priests in the Legionaries of Christ, all lying prostrate before the Holy Father. I had obtained some footage from this order to use in a Catholic video series, showing all these men, dressed in spotless white garments, lying face-down in total commitment to Christ. It was an awesome sight.

Joseph was deeply committed to God and his family. But that's not all. He was also committed to an interior life of prayer and spiritual growth – to the hidden life in Nazareth, calling no undue attention to himself. Will we do the same? Are we willing to forgo recognition? (I love what President Harry Truman once said: "It is amazing what you can accomplish if you do not care who gets the credit.") Are we willing to let go of our egos? Place no importance on possessions? Make prayer and interior growth our highest spiritual priorities?

Joseph was deeply **committed to God and his family.**

That's what real commitment is all about. Yet, sadly, it is seldom achieved. Remember the movie *Mr. Holland's Opus*, about the school teacher whose passion for music came at the expense of his deaf son? Mr. Holland certainly demonstrated commitment in one area, but while he touched the lives of many students his family relationships suffered. He didn't fulfill his primary commitment as a husband and father.

By contrast, look at how Joseph committed himself to work, family and

For many centuries, artwork often portrayed Joseph as an old man (most likely to defend the perpetual virginity of Mary). But today, we believe he married Mary in his late teens or early twenties — a customary age for a Jewish man.

faith. He remained steadfast in his focus on God, worked as an expression of love for his family, and created an atmosphere in the home for his son to grow into manhood. All the while seeking holiness in the "ordinariness" of life.

The interior life becomes all the more vibrant with fasting – not just abstaining from food, but from other pleasures in life, such as television, movies, magazines, recreation, especially sin… anything that places our focus on our own satisfaction instead of on God.

I'll never forget the Lenten season in which I gave up coffee – no easy task for someone who considers coffee to be far more than just a beverage, but a source of comfort akin to a warm blanket! The first week of Lent included withdrawals, headaches, lethargy and other ills. I would love to tell you that by Easter Sunday, I had kicked the coffee habit for good, but I would be lying. Truth is, I was ready to guzzle the brew straight from the carafe! But I survived. And I look back on that

Lenten season as a time of commitment. Fasting strengthens us in our resolve to avoid sin and follow Christ.

Joseph is a model of the virtue of prudence, which St. Thomas Aquinas describes as "right reason in action" – choosing to do what our conscience tells us to do. Prudence is living in the truth. If we act like we have our own "truth," then we are acting against prudence. We become imprudent.

> Joseph is a **model** of the virtue of prudence, which St. Thomas Aquinas describes as "right reason in action" – choosing to do what **moral reason** tells us to do.

The virtue of prudence is linked to the virtue of humility. Joseph accepts his position in the Holy Family as husband to Mary and father of Jesus. He only acts on what God has revealed to him. He doesn't try to be more than he is, nor does he accept being any less than he is. He knows who he is. Prudence is the middle ground between timidity and foolhardiness.

I think one of the greatest challenges we have as men is reasoning with our teenage children. Let's face it: we wonder sometimes when – or even if – they will ever arrive at the "age of reason." We're amazed at the logic – or lack thereof – of their arguments and defenses.

Take my teenage sons…please! Now, don't get me wrong – I love my boys, but sometimes I wonder if the hot Central California summers have over-heated their logic circuits. In this climate, driving in the car requires the non-stop use of the air-conditioner. It's not an option – it's a fact of life during our 100+ degree summers. Yet my sons will often argue that it's actually "cooler" driving with the windows down. They say that with the wind – hot as it is – blowing on their faces, they "feel" cooler than they do in the gentle currents of the air conditioner. I've tried reasoning, I've tried ranting, but all of my arguments have fallen on deaf (and hot!) ears. I've come to realize the importance of choosing which battles to fight and which battles to avoid engagement.

> Joseph had a **remarkable interior spirituality** – a genuine **peace of mind, soul** and heart.

Joseph not only shows us how to effectively communicate, but if we ask him, he will also intervene on our behalf with our kids to speak directly to their reason and intellect. Beyond

Joseph and Mary were called to marriage not by coincidence, but because it was God's plan that Jesus be born into a family — a plan which required Joseph and Mary to be married.

that, Joseph seeks the aid of Jesus, who has the tools we need to remain committed to the interior life and the virtue of prudence.

Joseph's interior life can be summed up in one word: God. God is the sole object of his thoughts and desires. The interior life is about the Kingdom of God within you, made even more holy by frequent reception of Holy Communion, undistracted from worldly affairs and material acquisitions, and focused on the possession of Christ.

Joseph had a remarkable interior spirituality – a genuine peace of mind, soul and heart. In life's burdens, divine grace is our bridge to a closer bond with Jesus. And Joseph can help us cross it. ∎

PRUDENCE

PART THREE

THE MISSION

God entrusted Joseph with an astonishing responsibility – leading, protecting and providing for the Holy Family. But, in the way we've come to expect from Joseph, he quietly accepted that responsibility with obedience and faithfulness. Now he humbly takes any attention we might lavish upon him, and directs it instead toward Christ. In fulfilling his unique mission, Joseph is seen in his completeness – God's "finished project" selected from the raw material of his humanity... lovingly crafted by God to follow His call... perfectly completed by grace, serving Jesus and Mary in all facets of his life. As men, we are called to live our own particular vocation and mission; to be all that God wants us to be (vocation) and do all that God wants us to do (mission). Joseph wants to help us prayerfully discover our identity as followers of Christ, fulfilling the Father's plan for our life. ■

MISSION

I could never be a jeweler or watch repairman, not because there's anything wrong with those jobs, but because I'd have to work with tiny tweezers, miniature screwdrivers and a myriad of microscopic parts, each smaller than the next. I don't deal well with things that little. Working with tiny tools requires sharp vision, fine dexterity and infinite patience…none of which I possess. Even tightening the screws on a pair of glasses pushes me over the edge.

Yet some people thrive on tackling tiny tasks: engravers, etchers, jewelers, watchmakers, eye surgeons, dentists and electronics technicians, to name but a few. God has gifted them differently than He gifted me. He has enabled me to speak in public without anxiety – something that causes many others to panic.

The point is, God has given us different gifts, abilities and temperaments. And He has given each of us a unique role to play in the greatest drama of all time: the saga of salvation. To gain a clearer picture of our special roles, we need to change our focus. Instead of telling God what *we* want from *Him*, we need to ask God how *He* wants *us* to use the gifts He has given us.

> The point is, **God has given us** different **gifts, abilities and temperaments.**

God equipped Joseph with the gifts He knew would be needed for his mission of caring for Mary and her child. God's divine plan was revealed to Joseph, and even though he wasn't the natural father of Jesus, he assumed the responsibility of becoming the living reflection of God the Father. In that sense, his mission is like our mission as fathers today.

Discovering our mission (purpose) in life gives us direction and brings glory to God in all that we think, say and do. Like Joseph, all are called to the general mission of sharing Christ with the world – the "Great Commission" given by Christ in Matthew 28. Joseph fulfilled that mission beautifully. He raised and shared Jesus with the world, bringing to adulthood the Word made flesh. We see this even at the birth of baby Jesus, with the visit of shepherds.

We are also called to a specific mission and purpose in life– one pre-ordained by God as the unique role He wants us to play in the story of salvation. This is our life's work – the specific use of God given skills, talents and virtues in serving Him within the home, the Church and the world.

Just as God gifted Joseph with the talents and virtues he needed to fulfill his mission, He will do no less for us.

And we can look to Joseph as the "master craftsman" who will show us how to use our gifts with patience and precision. We just need to ask for his help.

We are also called to a specific mission and purpose in life

At one point in my life, I had an avid interest in cars of the 1920s and '30s. I enjoyed the challenge of restoring these classics and ultimately ended up completing two projects from the ground up. In both cases, I relied on the knowledge and skills imparted to me by my father.

It's just like that with our Father in Heaven. He gives us the tools we need to get through the "projects" in our life – the difficulties we face, the relationships we have, the burdens we bear. All to help us complete the irreplaceable role He has chosen for us, and to help us grow closer to Him by grace along the path to eternal life.

Like Joseph, we have a choice in the matter. We have *freedom* - to get through life God's way or our way. We can only speculate on what would have occurred if Joseph had said "no" to God, to Mary and, ultimately, to Jesus. But he said "yes," and often repeated that affirmation as God's plan unfolded before him during the course of his life. How often do we say "no" to God? How often do we ask what we want from him instead

Joseph probably died before Jesus' public ministry. He is known as the patron saint of a "happy death" since he may well have died in the arms of Jesus and Mary.

of what He wants from us? If we are not looking for His will, it's doubtful we will find it – just like that old expression, "If you aim for nothing, you'll hit it every time."

How can we know God's will? We need to be open to external signs from people and situations (particularly spiritual direction), and internal guidance from the Holy Spirit (especially in prayer and reading Scripture.) We need to pattern ourselves after Joseph, who remained ever-vigilant for the voice of God. And we need to know that our mission doesn't necessarily require us to do "great" things for God. In fact, it is often in the ordinariness of daily living that our role in God's great plan is lived out. The effect we have on those around us can have eternal consequences. What we do to influence the present generation continues to affect future generations *and* has an impact on the eternal destination of their souls.

Today's culture pits pleasure against purpose, with a mantra that incessantly calls for pleasure in as many forms as possible. As you might expect, the quest for pleasure is never ending, never fulfilling and never satisfying. The search for purpose ultimately leads to God. And Joseph will help us find Him. ■

DIRECTION

HOPE

I'll never forget my first running event: a 10K loop through downtown Fresno. I was only mildly confident I would make it to the finish. I had been running a scant six months, going from "out of shape" to "somewhat improved shape," but nowhere close to what I would consider "10K running shape." As the crowd of runners started off, I had only one goal: making it across the finish line.

That goal was challenged right from the outset, as fast runners whizzed past me at a sub-seven-minute-mile pace. An obese man chugged past me, never letting up from the pounding rhythm of his heavy steps. There was even a runner that finished the event so early, he passed me running in the opposite direction back to the starting line! At long last, I finally did make it across the finish line… thanks to equal amounts of lung power, leg power and hope.

But there is another kind of hope; not in ourselves, but the hope we have in Christ – the desire for the Kingdom of Heaven and eternal life. It's rooted in the promises of Christ and it requires us to rely not on our own strength, but on the grace of the Holy Spirit.

> But there is another kind of hope; not in ourselves, but the hope we have in Christ

Did Joseph possess the virtue of hope? Without question. As a devout Jew and as a "just man" Joseph had the hope of Abraham who received abundant blessings by trusting in the promises of God – blessings that were fulfilled in Isaac and, ultimately, in Christ.

The Holy Spirit teaches us how to pray in hope. As we do so, God nourishes this virtue so that it grows. As hope increases, anxiety decreases.

While hope is the confident expectation of God's blessing and presence, it also carries with it the fear of offending God's love and incurring His punishment.

Sins against hope occur when we give in to despair or fail to trust in God's mercy and forgiveness - or when we start believing that we will obtain eternal life through our own merits.

> ## We can rely on Joseph to show us how to hope with confidence in Christ and His promises.

We can rely on Joseph to show us how to hope with confidence in Christ and His promises. Jesus will be there in troubled times, in illness, difficult relationships, emergencies, emotional problems and even our dying moments. Joseph will help us find Jesus and stay centered on Him.

In my profession, I have seen many cases where traumatic head injuries result in permanent brain damage. These often involve children. My heart goes out to these kids and their parents since the residual effects may include developmental delay, coordination problems and impairments in speech, memory, problem-solving and judgment.

You might tend to think the parents would lapse into hopelessness. But I've found the opposite to be true – often times, they are living examples of hope! They hope for improvement, for their children to return as close as possible to "normal." In particular,

Christian parents often display a steadfast hope that God will faithfully make all things new, and bring blessings into the difficult situations they face. Even with today's amazing medical advances, we are ultimately in God's hands and these Christian families know it. They have been a huge inspiration to me.

Hope allows us to persevere to the end of our days. Listen to the words of St. Teresa of Avila, who held a profound devotion to St. Joseph:

Hope, O my soul, hope. You know neither the day nor the hour. Watch carefully, for everything passes quickly, even though your impatience makes doubtful what is certain, and turns a very short time into a long one. Dream that the more you struggle, the more you prove the love that you bear your God, and the more you will rejoice one day with your Beloved, in a happiness and rapture that can never end.

In the military, I learned the importance of weaponry to protect myself and safeguard my fellow soldiers. Weapons not only repel attack, but take the offense against impending danger. Likewise, hope is also a weapon that protects us in the struggle for salvation (see 1 Thessalonians 5:8). One of the most powerful resources in our arsenal is the Holy Rosary, a meditation on the life of Jesus, Mary and Joseph combined with vocal prayer. The Rosary nourishes hope. Pray it daily, either in the traditional Marian way or using the St. Joseph Rosary in Appendix B (see page 74).

As a vocational rehabilitation consultant, I've become familiar with literally thousands of jobs and their requirements. And I've found one occupation that stands above the rest in terms of the knowledge, decision-making ability, life-and-death skills and stress involved. Know what it is?

Not an emergency room physician, air traffic controller or law enforcement officer. It's the carrier-based fighter pilot. Having met several of them over the years, I've become immensely impressed with the precise, ultra-vigilant attention they must possess in order to fulfill their mission.

The fighter pilot is brutally catapult-ed from the carrier deck, accelerating

> The **fighter pilot** is brutally catapulted from the carrier deck, accelerating from zero to 165 miles per hour **in less** than two **seconds!** But it's the landing that is **most impressive.**

from zero to 165 miles per hour in less than two seconds! But it's the landing that is most impressive. The pilot must hit the carrier deck at precisely the right location, angle and speed to snag one of four arresting cables with the tailhook. Doing this on a carrier that is moving forward, pitching up and down over a windy sea, with a landing deck that doesn't line up with the car-rier's direction of movement, is incred-ibly difficult. Add darkness or bad weather, and you've got the ultimate white-knuckle experience! But with assistance from radar, guidance sys-tems and the carrier crew, fighter pilots successfully accomplish this superhu-man challenge on a daily basis.

Our hope in the Lord is much like this. Our goal is to "land" safely in God's eternal kingdom, relying on His "guidance system" of hope and prayer. Challenging? Yes. Attainable? Absolutely! ∎

TRUST

As a Jew, Joseph saw to it that Jesus was circumcised on the eigth day (possibly even performing the rite himself). He also demonstrated faith and obedience by naming the child "Jesus," following the words of the angel.

WORK

When I started my vocational rehabilitation practice in 1976, I had no office, no employees...not even a desk. I literally worked out of the trunk of my car, transporting files, test materials and note pads from one client's home to another. A bare-bones beginning to be sure. But in His Providence, God blessed what I was doing and ultimately gave me a comfortable office, a terrific staff and, yes, even a real desk! Many doors have opened for me since then, all by the grace of God.

The way I see it, I'm still serving an "apprenticeship" in my work. I don't just mean my job, but all aspects of my life, including my relationships with my family, the Church and the community. There's always a new challenge or twist to the daily situations around me that call for new and creative ways to use what God has given me. Do you still see yourself as an apprentice?

> He understands that **labor** is a way of **participating** in the work of **creation** and redemption.

For us "apprentice workers," there is no one better to learn from than Joseph, the Patron of Workers. He's in Heaven right now to guide us on earth: in *what* work we should do and *how* we should do it with the skills and abilities we have received. In Christ, he is the ultimate vocational guidance counselor because he understands that labor is a way of participating in the work of creation and redemption.

As noted by Pope John Paul II, **"Work was the daily expression of love in the life of the Family of Nazareth"** (*Redemptoris Custos*, #22).

St. Teresa of Avila said that while other saints have specific patronages, we can pray to St. Joseph in any need. She greatly influenced the Church by promoting devotion to St. Joseph.

We men often allow ourselves to be defined by the work we do. It's usually the first thing we ask when we meet somebody new: "What kind of work do you do?" But if we limit our identity (and the identities of others) to our job description, we limit the options for who we are in a broader sense. God gave us skills, talents and virtues to use wherever we find ourselves - whether it's the workplace, home, church or in volunteer pursuits. Even if we are unemployed, our identity in Christ remains intact.

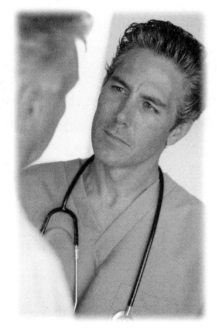

Like Joseph, our work gives us a way of fulfilling our mission in Christ. Devotion to Joseph allows us to be better equipped mentally, physically and spiritually for whatever working situations we encounter.

Like Joseph, our work gives us a way of fulfilling our mission in Christ.

I have counted on Joseph many times to fill the deficiencies I leave as husband, father and friend. He helps us honor the gifts we have received from our Creator, and collaborate with the redemptive work of Christ.

To follow Joseph is to seek balance between work and family, between our job and home, between day commitments and evening commitments.

As a husband and the father of four sons and a daughter, the issue of balance is one I'm still struggling with. I spent years in Catholic Scouting with my boys, which requires taking time for weekly troop meetings, monthly campouts, merit badges, religious emblem instruction and committee meetings. Then there is my daughter – I need to be involved with her, too. Oh, and my wife. Where does she fit in? Plus I've got my day job, and in my "spare time" I write Catholic books and produce Catholic videos. Then there are my interests in old cars, electric trains, antiques and model-building. I need help!

And I find it through trusting Joseph and the son he trained, Jesus. They help me sort out my priorities, and miraculously make time for me to lead a balanced (if busy!) life. ∎

SKILLS

FAMILY

Living in an agricultural area of California affords our family many unique opportunities, not the least of which is finding our way through the annual "corn maze" each October. Take a few acres of tall corn stalks, plow out a maze with lots of twists, turns and dead ends, and you've got a corn maze. Maybe that's why Native Americans call it "maize"?

When my daughter was 7, one of her friends held a birthday party at the local corn maze. At the appointed time, kids and their parents entered the corn maze and began looking for five numbered sign posts to guide them from one clue to the next and, eventually, the exit. Simple, right? Well… two hours after the starting time, most of the guests were *still* trapped in the maze. On top of that, the sun had set and it was now pitch black! It took outside help from a so-called "corn cop" for us to finally find our way out.

> He **defends** us from the wedge that Satan **often tries** to drive between **family** members.

Family life is a lot like that. We enter it without instructions and we try and work our way through its maze of twists, turns and dead ends. But like the "corn cop," Joseph is right there, ready to show us how to navigate our families through it all.

One of Joseph's title is Protector of the Church. Since the Church is the family of God, the family itself is considered the "domestic church," the Church in miniature. So Joseph's protection extends to our families as well as the Church at large. He defends us from the wedge that Satan often tries to drive between family members. The enemy has a particular interest in destroying Christian families – those which take their faith seriously – and he will create whatever disruption is necessary to accomplish his goal. But Joseph will defend us, living up to another of his many titles: Pillar of Family Life.

I will always remember the challenge of teaching each of my five children how to ride a bicycle. No two of them learned at the same age – some began riding as early as age 4, while others didn't learn until age 6. Each learned their own way, at their own pace. I remember running alongside my kids as their bikes would weave and wobble down the sidewalk, reminding them to pedal - since without power, there is no chance of moving forward. There were falls, scrapes and tears along the way, but they didn't deter me from offering guidance and praise. Eventually, each of my children became fully independent and confident in the ability to ride a bicycle.

What a great illustration of family life! It takes power to keep a family moving forward in its faith – the power of prayer, the Church and the Sacraments. It takes guidance and encouragement to keep a family on track, and Joseph provides them in abundance when we seek him. There may be bumps and tumbles along the way, but God's love is always there to surround us and set us straight.

Love is what the family is all about. Pope John Paul II has described the family as a cradle of life and love, the place in which individuals are born and grown. He says the family is to society what the cell is to a living organism – the basic building block.

Joseph was born in Palestine, where the country of Israel is located today.

It's the family's mission to be a community of life and love; to guard, reveal and communicate love. The family is a reflection of God's love for His people and Christ's love for His Church. And just as Joseph daily demonstrated his love for the Holy Family, so will he help today's families as we seek to become more and more what we can and should be as members of God's Kingdom on earth.

> The **family** is a reflection of God's love for His people and Christ's **love** for His **Church.**

Joseph knows how to make a house a holy place, and those within it a holy family. He wants Jesus to be the center of our homes and the center of each life dwelling within. Jesus gives families eternal perspective so that all that is done and said has eternal consequences, for better or for worse. (To learn more about the family's mission and purpose, see my book *The Mission of the Catholic Family: On the Pathway to Heaven*).

Three brothers were discussing their recently deceased father whom they loved very much. All the first son wanted from his father's personal belongings was his ring, a lifetime reminder of his dad. The second son wanted his father's watch for the same reason. But the third son made an odd request. He asked for his father's canceled checks. He wanted to see how his dad spent his money.

We all leave a legacy. Does our faith in God show in every part of our lives – even in the checkbook registers we leave behind?

It is believed that Joseph died before Jesus and Mary, yet what a rich legacy he left them – a legacy of endless examples showing who he was as a man of God.

What will be our legacy? We build it with each new day. Let's allow Joseph to help with the construction. ∎

REVEAL

Joseph was a descendant of Abraham from the line of King David — the royal line from which the Messiah would come — making him an heir to God's promise of deliverance.

JESUS

I learned a lot at my father's workbench. He was the consummate "tool guy" who could build or repair just about anything. He was versatile, too, working confidently with wood and metal, cars and trucks, plumbing and electricity. Because of him, I became fascinated with tools in my childhood. Dad showed me their purpose and how to use them, everything from pliers to wrenches, ball peen hammers to sockets. But to me, the granddaddy of all tools had to be the torque wrench – a long-handled, socket turning lever that displayed the amount of torque (twisting force) being applied to a nut or bolt. I thought that 18-inch beauty was by far the coolest tool in my dad's workshop.

Then one weekend, I discovered that there were much larger, cooler members of the torque wrench family. My dad took me to the truck repair shop where he worked, and I wandered through the facility until I caught sight of a tool so huge, so impressive, so impossibly cool, it stopped me dead in my tracks: a gleaming, double-handled torque wrench *over 4 feet long*. A wrench so enormous, my dad explained, it took *two men* to turn it. For this 10-year-old, discovering that enormous torque wrench was a life-altering experience!

...Joseph's protection extends to our families as well as the Church at large.

Joseph and my dad had a lot in common. Just as my father would often teach me about tools, Joseph would have instructed Jesus in their use. This father-son relationship no doubt lasted from Jesus' childhood to the time of Joseph's death, which probably took place before Jesus began his public ministry.

If we want to know, love and serve Christ more completely, then we can learn from the one man who spent more time with Jesus than any other: his chosen father. Joseph not only taught Jesus, but got to know him more intimately than any other Saint in the Kingdom of Heaven, with the exception of Mary. And like any son, Jesus would likely have acquired some of the characteristics of both His parents.

Some call Joseph the "foster father" of Jesus. But "chosen father" is more accurate, since a foster father doesn't enter the child's life until after the child is born.

Even though my father was alive for only the first 15 years of my life, he is still a big part of who I am: my personality, my disposition, my general nature…even my quirks. In a real sense, I have "become" my father. And in the same way, in His human nature, Jesus was like Joseph. He drew from Joseph's knowledge and fatherly role. They had a close, intimate relationship; an inseparable bond. Joseph was an image of God the Father. He exer-

cised his fatherhood at the service of and as an instrument of the divine Fatherhood.

When we go to Joseph, he doesn't keep our devotion to himself. Instead, he directs our attention to his son. In a mysterious way, we can experience eternity <u>now</u> through the presence of Jesus, especially in the Holy Eucharist.

He is found in prayer, word and sacrament – the direct link between our existence in time to Christ's existence in eternity.

He is found in the Mass, as the sacred consecration of the bread and wine becomes the most Precious Body and Blood of Jesus, indwelling in us as we receive Holy Communion.

He is found in His Word, the Scriptures. In Armenian, "Bible" is translated "breath of God," and surely it is. Joseph knew this in a special way, as he literally heard and felt his son's breath since His infancy – the breath of God.

He is found in the Sacrament of Reconciliation. His sacrifice on the cross offers forgiveness and opens the gates of Heaven. Joseph will guide us in the examination of our conscience so that a good confession will result in healing our brokenness.

Nowadays, I have the joy of teaching my own kids about tools. Not just the tools in my workshop, but tools of a more important and eternal nature – the tools for faith and life. For the times I failed to give them the tools they need, or when they reject what I have to offer, I know I can count on my favorite contractor, Joseph of Nazareth, for backup. ■

MARY

In the movie, *The Passion of the Christ,* Mary is portrayed as mother to both Jesus and His disciples. I will always remember that portrayal, in which Mary is seen as full of sorrow, but strong in her complete surrender to God's will. And while I enjoyed the power and artistry of the movie, I found myself secretly hoping that at least one of the flashback sequences would include Joseph. I wanted to see him interact with Jesus and Mary, since he was the man destined for greatness through his humble, ordinary and deeply spiritual life.

Joseph gave his entire self to Mary and Jesus. He had the privilege of being married to the most grace-filled woman that God could provide as mother for His Son. He was united with her forever in the bond of mar-riage and must have shared in her deep interior life and virtues.

For some, it may not be considered "manly" to have a Marian devotion. Yet this woman endured hardships, sorrow and agony that most men would shrink from. More importantly, she lovingly offers the safe, maternal refuge of her Immaculate Heart. She wants to be there for us guys when we need her spiritual maternity and deep love.

Mary would also be the first to encourage devotion to her spouse, Joseph. She knows he is the man that God hand-picked to be her spouse and to be the earthly father of Jesus. And she knows what a good teacher he is. She saw him teach Jesus many times, and she has seen how well he can teach youth and other men. She and young Jesus were entrusted to his care, and she shared much in common with her dear husband, especially their mutual vocation and mission to create the family life needed for the Son of God to grow into manhood and enter his public ministry.

In addition to the Bible, we can understand more about Joseph by studying the Church's official teachings, the Litany of St. Joseph, Apostolic Tradition, the Liturgy and the saints devoted to him.

Through the years, I have interviewed many people for my various video projects. Yet one quote from *Joseph: The Man Closest to Christ* stands among my favorites: "The Rosary is not a tool, it's a weapon." A powerful truth, made even more profound by the fact that it came from Lt. Col. Thomas VaVerka, who said it while standing before a huge mural of an Apache attack helicopter! As he said it, I couldn't help but agree with him that the Rosary is like a heavily-armed gunship ready to lock on to Satan and take him out; every bead a silver bullet.

"The Rosary is not a tool, it's a weapon."

One of the best things we ever did as a family was join three other families in a monthly Rosary group. Hearing 20 adults and children praying the Rosary aloud must be very pleasing to the Blessed Mother. It sure has been for me. As Pope Leo XIII (1889) and Pope John Paul II (1989) have asked, Joseph should be remembered at the end of the Rosary by a special prayer written by Pope Leo XIII (see Appendix B, page 77).

I'm sure Joseph increased in holiness by his daily companionship with Mary. Together, Joseph and Mary will show couples what it takes to grow in personal holiness and how to strengthen their marriage bond. As a husband,

I'm called to do everything I can to help my wife get to Heaven (and vice-versa). I've got to be "Joseph" to her and she's got to be "Mary" to me.

As husbands, we must create a home environment that allows the love between spouses to be modeled for (and witnessed by) our children. We can do this so much more effectively with the help of the world's greatest husband: Joseph. Through his example and intercession, we'll acquire a profound devotion to Mary and, through her, to Jesus. We'll discover more and more the purpose and plan God has designed for us.

Joseph and Mary reveal the two greatest vocation stories of all time, and they will help us discover our own personal vocation and mission as well.

My mother is Italian, a first-generation descendant from the small Northern Italian town of Lucca. Over the years, she has had the joys and pains that most mothers experience, including the loss of her beloved husband at an early age (he was 50, she was 43). She has seen her two sons become men and enter marriage and family life. And she has experienced the wonder of grandchildren. Throughout all of this, she has held a steady focus on the Sacramental life in the Church, on daily prayer and service to others. She reminds me of Mary.

These qualities are a template for how we should live our lives – stay focused on Christ, on His Church, and on helping those in need, with kindness and humility. Joseph is the perfect fellow to help us acquire these qualities, and find Mary in the process. ■

EVIL

One of the big events in the life of a Cub Scout is the annual Space Derby, in which propeller-driven "spaceships" race one another along parallel strings stretched high across the room. Having four sons, I've helped each of them construct a wide variety of cosmic cruisers over the years.

One particular spaceship really stands out. My son and I spent a great deal of time carefully shaping the styrofoam body with the ultimate in precision designer tools: a potato peeler. Unfortunately, we should have taken more time choosing the paint for our spacecraft. We simply grabbed a convenient can of spray lacquer, took aim and fired away with a blast of paint…which immediately melted the styrofoam into a crispy, shapeless blob. We went from "Star Trek" to "star wreck" at warp speed.

But we learned a lesson about the relationship between the fragile body of a styrofoam spaceship and the destructive power of lacquer paint. It's a lot like our relationship with sin, in which our otherwise Christ-like image becomes distorted and corrupt when sin touches us with its toxicity. But unlike styrofoam, we can repent and be re-formed in the image of Christ, through the forgiveness and grace of God, especially in confession.

I think back to Joseph's workshop where he almost surely repaired broken furniture to be used again by the working class residents of Nazareth. He probably also saw lives broken down by evil and sin, and now calls us to his son, Jesus, so that our brokenness can be repaired.

One of my favorite titles for Joseph is "Terror of Demons" - and indeed, he is a bold protector from the evil spirits that prowl throughout the world. Just as he protected the Child Jesus from the Enemy, so will he keep us out of harm's way, if we ask for his help.

"Terror of demons" is one of Joseph's key titles, recognizing his responsibility for protecting Jesus (and the Body of Christ, the Church) from forces that would attempt to destroy Him.

However, we must not doubt Satan's commitment and resolve to destroy those who believe in Christ. He will tempt us with the glossy attraction of magazines, movies and media, with the so-called "adult" content found on computers and cable channels, and with the promise of pleasure from possessions and power.

St. Ignatius of Loyola said that there are three voices within us: the voice of Satan who longs to destroy us, to make certain we are self-centered and prideful; the voice of ourselves, manifested by our thoughts, words, emotions and actions; and finally, the voice of God who loves us completely, 100% of the time, and wants us to achieve eternal life in Heaven.

Which voice do we hear? It's probably a mixture of all three voices. When we hear the voice of evil, we have the option to immediately invoke the protection of Joseph. He will rebuke Satan and surround us with his cloak of goodness and virtue.

The by-product of our wrongdoing is often guilt, sorrow and anxiety. This occurs when we cross the threshold of temptation, moving from good to bad. Sometimes we flirt with temptation, thinking we can "check it out" without actually going all the way into the realm of sin. But Jesus knew our frailty when he included "lead us not into temptation" in the Lord's Prayer.

To avoid sin, we must avoid the occasions or circumstances that can lead to sin. It is not in our power to avoid all temptation (Jesus, too, was tempted), but we can stay away from *unnecessary* temptation. Maybe our computer password should be "Joseph" to remind us of his intent to protect!

If we're trapped in habitual sin, then we need to stop – to just say "no." I realize this is much easier said than done, but with the protective mantle of Joseph and the saving grace of Christ, we can break free from the clamp of evil. With some types of habitual sin, particularly addictions, healing is often necessary. We've been "hard-wired" to the same repeated failings. Consistent prayer and frequent Sacramental confession will help release the vice that the Evil One places on those entwined in patterns of repetitive sin.

In the past few years, I've had to change my diet, breaking free from chips, diet soft drinks…even caffeine. I had achieved "world class" status in my consumption of these items and, like sin, they were daily reminders of how habits can become deeply ingrained. Frequent confession will help erase the repetitive sins on the mental list that we carry to the priest. Thanks be to God for this channel of grace and healing that connects us with Christ in the Sacrament of Reconciliation.

Joseph will guide you in first recognizing the presence of evil and vice, then give you an express ticket directly to his son Jesus, so that His saving Blood can wash away your sins. ■

CONFESSION

> *"At the workbench where he plied*
> *his trade together with Jesus,*
> *Joseph brought human work closer to*
> *the mystery of the Redemption."*
>
> Pope John Paul II
> *(Redemptoris Custos, #22)*

CONCLUSION

I hope you have drawn closer to Joseph at the "workbench" found in these pages. It you have, then he will bring you closer to Jesus, who in turn guides you to eternal life.

Joseph accomplishes this task with great love for each one of us. If we accept Joseph as our guardian and patron, then we accept his God-given role and become his "building project." But he does more than help us build our lives – he also shows us how to help others build their lives in Christ. He helps us love and honor our spouses and raise good children, so they will become true sons and daughters of Christ. In fact, if we don't teach real manhood to our children as shown by Joseph's example, then, by default, the world will convey its definition – one that pitches superficial masculinity in the form of pleasure, power and possessions.

Joseph is a master craftsman in God's workshop of human life! It is the trade he knows best. And we can choose to be his student-apprentices. He will never fail us or let us down:

Joseph will *pray* for us. He is a powerful intercessor on our behalf and will go to his son, Jesus, with our needs.

Joseph will *lead* us in prayer and show us how to pray, often using silence as his classroom, so that we can better hear God's call. We can learn how to go beyond asking for God's help in our needs – and move to adoration, thanksgiving, praise, listening and contemplating Christ in Sacred Scripture and devotions (i.e. Sacred Heart of Jesus, Immaculate Heart of Mary).

Joseph will *teach* us what we need to learn about life, such as purity of body, mind and spirit, the value of simplicity and responsibility. He is the model of authentic manhood and will show us what it means to be a man of God, an important reality for *both* men and women to understand.

Joseph will *guide* us in and through situations, events and relationships. As a devoted father, he will be there when we need him and will watch over us with his kind heart united to the heart of Mary, his spouse.

Joseph will *equip* us with the skills we need to get through life, particularly in raising children. Joseph knows what we need, and will see that our needs are met.

Joseph will *protect* us from the Devil and from sins of the flesh. Known as the Terror of Demons, he is a most capable adversary of Satan and is fully prepared to take him on with no hesitation or fear.

Joseph will work with us, side-by-side, not just in our job, but in all that comprises our lifework in the home, church and world. Pope John Paul II reminds us that, "Work was the daily expression of love in the life of the Family of Nazareth" (John Paul II *Redemptoris Custos,* #22), and so should it be for us. The use of our talents and skills can be expressions of love that bring glory to God – whether we use those talents and skills in the home, the workplace, the Church, the world or in any other relationship or setting.

Joseph will help with us, achieve those Christ-like virtues that place us on high moral ground, far above the worldly promotion of "self," seeking *purpose*, not pleasure. Pope John Paul II reminds us: "St. Joseph is the model of those humble ones that Christianity raises up to great destinies... he is the proof that in order to be a good and genuine follower of Christ, there is no need of great things – it is enough to have the common, simple and human virtues, but they need to be true and authentic." (John Paul II *Redemptoris Custos,* #24).

That's the Joseph I know. My prayer is that you will fully embrace the example that flows from him and the abundant blessings that flow through him. May you discover that he is, indeed, "not your average Joe."

Let him *pray* for you.
Let him *lead* you in prayer.
Let him *teach* you about virtues.
Let him *guide* you through life.
Let him *equip* you with the skills you need.
Let him *protect* you from evil.
Let him *work* with you.

Go to Joseph!

AFTERWORD

I have a confession to make. The words you've just finished reading were not intended only for you. I intended them for myself also, because *I* need to be reminded, encouraged and motivated daily to be more like the man God wants *me* to be.

Hopefully they will help you, too, as you grow in your devotion to St. Joseph and achieve a level of manhood that embraces his virtuous life. Remember, St. Joseph knows a lot about tools and how to use them – how to help the men of this world grow in their faith through the abundant life of grace that flows from Jesus Christ.

I've never known St. Joseph to fail in response to my prayers. ∎

SCRIPTURAL REFERENCES TO ST. JOSEPH

Joseph mentioned by name:

Matthew 1:16, 18, 19, 20, 24; 2:13, 19.
Luke 1:27; 2:4, 16; 3:23; 4:22.
John 1:45; 6:42.

Titles of Betrothed, Husband and Wife applied to Joseph and Mary:

Matthew 1:16, 18, 19, 20, 24.
Luke 1:27; 2:5.

Titles of Parent, Father and Son applied to Joseph and Jesus:

Matthew 13:55.
Luke 2:27, 33, 41, 43, 48; 3:23; 4:22.
John 1:45; 6:42.

Joseph in relation to David:

Matthew 1:20 (1:1-17).
Luke 1:27; 2:4 (1:32, 69; 2:11; 3:23-31)

Joseph associated with Nazareth:

Matthew 2:23.
Luke 1:26; 2:4, 39, 51 (4:16-22).
John 1:45-46.

Justice and Obedience of Joseph:

Matthew 1:19, 24; 2:14, 21, 22.
Luke 2:4, 22-24, 39

Joseph the Carpenter:

Matthew 13:55 (Mark 6:3).

Reprinted with permission from *Joseph in the New Testament*
by Fr. Larry Toschi, OSJ, pages 109-110.
Available from Guardian of the Redeemer Publications,
544 W. Cliff Dr., Santa Cruz, CA 95060-6147,
(831) 457-1868, toll free (866) MARELLO, www.osjoseph.org.

PRAYERS TO ST. JOSEPH

PRAYER OF POPE LEO XIII TO ST. JOSEPH
(TO BE SAID AFTER THE ROSARY)

To you, O Blessed Joseph, we come in our trials, and having asked the help of your most holy spouse, we confidently ask your patronage also. Through that Sacred bond of charity which united you to the Immaculate Virgin Mother of God and through the fatherly love with which you embraced the Child Jesus, we humbly beg you to look graciously upon the beloved inheritance which Jesus Christ purchased by his blood, and to aid us in our necessities with your power and strength.

O most provident guardian of the Holy Family, defend the chosen children of Jesus Christ. Most beloved father, dispel the evil of falsehood and sin. Our most mighty protector, graciously assist us from heaven in our struggle with the powers of darkness. And just as you once saved the Child Jesus from mortal danger, so now defend God's Holy Church from the snares of her enemies and from all adversity. Shield each one of us by your constant protection, so that, supported by your example and your help, we may be able to live a virtuous life, to die a holy death, and to obtain eternal happiness in heaven. **Amen.**

PRAYER OF PIUS X TO ST. JOSEPH THE WORKER

Glorious St. Joseph, model of all who work, obtain for me the grace to work conscientiously, putting the call of duty above my many sins; to work with gratitude and joy, considering it an honor to employ and develop, by my labor, the gifts received from God; to work with order, peace, moderation and patience, never recoiling before weariness or difficulties; to work, above all, with pure intention and detachment from self, having always before my eyes death and the account which I must then render of time lost, of talents wasted, of good omitted, and of vain complacency in success, so fatal to the work of God. All for Jesus, all through Mary, all in imitation of you, O patriarch Joseph. This shall be my motto in life and death. **Amen.**

ST. JOSEPH ROSARY

May be prayed just as Marian rosary, substituting the following prayer for the "Hail Mary":

Joseph, son of David, and husband of Mary; we honor you, guardian of the Redeemer, and we adore the Child you named Jesus. Saint Joseph, patron of the universal Church, pray for us, that like you, we may live totally dedicated to the interests of the Savior.

Mysteries

1. Betrothal to Mary (Mt 1:18).
2. Annunciation to Joseph (Mt 1:19-21).
3. Birth and Naming of Jesus (Mt 1:22-25).
4. Flight to Egypt (Mt 2:13-15).
5. Hidden Life at Nazareth (Mt 2:23; Lk 2:51-52).

ST. JOSEPH NOVENA
OPENING PRAYER TO ST. JOSEPH FOR FAITH:

Blessed St. Joseph, heir of all the patriarchs, obtain for me this beautiful and precious virtue. Give me a lively faith, which is the foundation of all holiness, that faith without which no one can be pleasing to God. Obtain for me a faith that triumphs over all the temptations of the world and conquers human respect; a faith that cannot be shaken and that seeks God alone. In imitation of you, make me live by faith and submit my mind and heart to God, so that one day I may behold in Heaven what I now firmly believe on earth. **Amen.**

DAY ONE:
**The Annunciation
to the Betrothed Just Man**

First reading: Matthew 1:18-21
Second reading: John Paul II, *Redemptoris Custos*, sections 2-3
One or more decades of the St. Joseph Rosary (prayed as Marian Rosary, substituting "Hail Mary" with "Joseph, Son of David"):

Joseph, son of David, and husband of Mary; we honor you, guardian of the Redeemer, and we adore the child you named Jesus. Saint Joseph, patron of the universal church, pray for us, that like you, we may live totally dedicated to the interests of the Savior.

DAY TWO:
Joseph Takes Mary His Wife

First reading: Matthew 1:24
Second reading: John Paul II, *Redemptoris Custos*, section 20

- One or more decades of the St. Joseph Rosary

DAY THREE:
The Birth and Naming of Jesus, Son of David

First reading: Matthew 1:16, 25
Second reading: John Paul II,
Redemptoris Custos, sections 10, 12

- One or more decades
  of the St. Joseph Rosary

DAY FOUR:
The Presentation of Jesus, According to the Law of the Lord

First reading: Luke 2:22-40
Second reading: John Paul II,
Redemptoris Custos, section 13

- One or more decades
  of the St. Joseph Rosary

DAY FIVE:
The Flight into Egypt

First reading: Matthew 2:13-15
Second reading: John Paul II,
Redemptoris Custos, section 14

- One or more decades
  of the St. Joseph Rosary

DAY SIX:
The Finding in the Temple and the Fatherhood of Joseph

First reading: Luke 2:41-52
Second reading: John Paul II,
Redemptoris Custos, section 8

- One or more decades
  of the St. Joseph Rosary

DAY SEVEN:
Joseph the Worker

First reading: Matthew 13:53-55a
Second reading: John Paul II,
Redemptoris Custos, sections 22, 24

- One or more decades
  of the St. Joseph Rosary

DAY EIGHT:
Patron of the Hidden and Interior Life

First reading: Colossians 3:1-4
Second reading: John Paul II,
Redemptoris Custos, sections 25-27d

- One or more decades
  of the St. Joseph Rosary

DAY NINE:
Patron and Model of the Church

First reading: 1 Corinthians 12:12, 27
Second reading: John Paul II,
Redemptoris Custos, section 28, 30

- One or more decades
  of the St. Joseph Rosary

NOTE: *Redemptoris Custos* is also available from Guardian of the Redeemer publications (831) 457-1868, toll free (866) MARELLO, www.osjoseph.org.

LITANY OF ST. JOSEPH

Lord, have mercy
Lord, have mercy
Christ, have mercy
Christ, have mercy
Lord, have mercy
Lord, have mercy
God our Father in Heaven
have mercy on us
God the Son, Redeemer of the world
have mercy on us
God the Holy Spirit
have mercy on us
Holy Trinity, one God
have mercy on us
Holy Mary
pray for us
Saint Joseph
pray for us
Noble son of the House of David
pray for us
Light of patriarchs
pray for us
Husband of the Mother of God
pray for us
Guardian of the Virgin
pray for us
Foster father of the Son of God
pray for us
Faithful guardian of Christ
pray for us
Head of the holy family
pray for us
Joseph, chaste and just
pray for us
Joseph, prudent and brave
pray for us

Joseph, obedient and loyal
pray for us
Pattern of patience
pray for us
Lover of poverty
pray for us
Model of workers
pray for us
Example to parents
pray for us
Guardian of virgins
pray for us
Pillar of family life
pray for us
Comfort of the troubled
pray for us
Hope of the sick
pray for us
Patron of the dying
pray for us
Terror of evil spirits
pray for us
Protector of the Church
pray for us
Lamb of God, you take
away the sins of the world
have mercy on us
Lamb of God, you take
away the sins of the world
have mercy on us
Lamb of God, you take
away the sins of the world
have mercy on us
God made him master
of his household
*And put him in charge
of all that he owned*

Let us pray: God, in Your infinite wisdom and love, You chose Joseph to be the husband of Mary, the Mother of your Son. May we have the help of his prayers in Heaven and enjoy his protection on earth. We ask this through Christ our Lord. **Amen.**

THE SEVEN SORROWS AND JOYS OF ST. JOSEPH

1. *Chaste Lover of Mary, how overwhelmed you were when you thought that you would have to end your betrothal to her. But when the angel of God came to you in a dream, you were filled with awe to realize that Mary would be your wife, and you would be the guardian of the Messiah.*
Help us St. Joseph, help our families and all our loved ones to overcome all sadness of heart and develop an absolute trust in God's goodness.

2. *Faithful guardian of Jesus, what a failure you thought you were when you could only provide a stable for the birth of the Holy Child. And then what a wonder it was when shepherds came to tell of angel choirs, and the Wise Men came to adore the King of Kings.*
Through your example and prayers, help us St.Joseph and all we love to become like sinless mangers where the Savior of the world may be received with absolute love and respect.

3. *Tender-hearted Joseph, you too felt pain when the Blood of Jesus was first shed at His circumcision. Yet how proud you were to be the one privileged to give the Name of Jesus, Savior, to the very Son of God.*
Pray for us St. Joseph, that the Sacred Blood of Christ, poured out for our salvation, may guard our families, so the divine Name of Jesus may be written in our hearts forever.

4. *Joseph, loving husband, how bewildered you were when Simeon spoke the words of warning that the hearts of Jesus and Mary would be pierced with sorrows. Yet his prediction that this would lead to the salvation of innumerable souls filled you with consolation.*
Help us, St. Joseph, to see with eyes of faith that even the sorrows and pains of those we deeply love can become the pathway to salvation and eternal life.

5. *Courageous protector of the Holy Family, how terrified you were when you had to make the sudden flight with Jesus and Mary to escape the treachery of King Herod and the cruelty of his soldiers. But when you reached Egypt, what satisfaction you had to know that the Savior of the world had come to replace the pagan idols.*
Teach us by your example, St. Joseph, to keep far from the false idols of earthly attractions, so that like you, we may be entirely devoted to the service of Jesus and Mary.

6. *Ever-obedient Joseph, you trustingly returned to Nazareth at God's command, in spite of your fear that King Herod's son might still be a threat to Jesus' life. Then what fatherly pride you had in seeing Jesus grow in wisdom and grace before God and men under your care.* Show us St. Joseph, how to be free from all useless fear and worry, so we may enjoy the peace of a tranquil conscience, living safely with Jesus and Mary in our hearts.

7. *Dependable father and husband, how frantic you and Mary were when, through no fault of yours, you searched for three days to find Jesus. What incredible relief was yours when you found Him safe in the Temple of God.* Help us St. Joseph, never to lose Jesus through the fault of our own sins. But if we should lose Him, lead us back with unwearied sorrow, until we find Him again; so that we, like you, may finally pass from this life, dying safely in the arms of Jesus and Mary.

And Jesus Himself, when he began His work, was about thirty years old being, as was supposed, the son of Joseph.

Pray for us, holy Joseph.
That we may be made worthy of the promises of Christ.

Let us pray:
Blessed St. Joseph, tender-hearted father, faithful guardian of Jesus, chaste spouse of the Mother of God, I pray and beseech you to offer to God the Father my praise to Him through His divine Son, who died on the Cross and rose again to give us sinners new life. Through the Holy Name of Jesus, pray with us that we may obtain from the eternal Father, the favor we ask…(Pause)… We have been unfaithful to the unfailing love of God the Father; beg of Jesus' mercy for us. Amid the splendors of God's loving Presence, do not forget the sorrows of those who suffer, those who pray, those who weep. By your prayers and those of your most holy spouse, our Blessed Lady, may the love of Jesus answer our call of confident hope. **Amen.**

These prayers and others are from the *Family of St. Joseph Prayer Manual* (3rd edition), available from Guardian of the Redeemer Publications, 544 W. Cliff Dr., Santa Cruz, CA 95060-6147, (831) 457-1868, toll free (866) MARELLO, www.osjoseph.org.

APPENDIX C

THE OBLATES OF ST. JOSEPH

The Oblates of St. Joseph are a Religious Order of priests and brothers founded by St. Joseph Marello in 1878 in Italy. He was inspired to gather a group of young men who desired to consecrate themselves to the love and service of Jesus in imitation of the prayerful, humble and dedicated example of St. Joseph.

St. Marello proposed a high ideal of an intense spiritual life united with a tremendous spirit of service. He viewed St. Joseph as a pathway to holiness in which we can become "extraordinary in ordinary things," keeping before us the image of the young Jesus – simple, poor and hidden away, working for our salvation through the toil of everyday life. Joseph Marello was canonized on November 25, 2001.

The Oblates of St. Joseph serve Jesus in whatever work is most necessary, without seeking to draw attention to themselves, working solely for the love of Christ. St. Marello desired that they remain open to whatever missions divine Providence sends their way, particularly assisting local churches most in need, the Christian education of young people, and leading people to Christ through the example of St. Joseph. They began as a small community, but have gradually grown and spread.

In 1915, the Holy Father requested that the Oblates of St. Joseph start their apostolic services abroad, carrying devotion and the spirit of St. Joseph throughout the world. At present, they are working in the following countries:

Bolivia	Brazil	Nigeria	India	Italy
Mexico	Peru	Philippines	Poland	United States

The Oblates serve Christ through:

1. Spreading devotion to St. Joseph

2. Loyalty to the Holy Father and the teachings of the Catholic Church

3. Pastoral work in areas having lack of clergy

4. Christian formation and guidance of young people

5. Religious education

6. Catholic schools

7. Serving the elderly, immigrants and the poor

8. Spiritual direction for retreats

9. Foreign missions

Lay Associates

Associates to the Oblates of St. Joseph are lay men and women (and priests) without profession of vows, who choose to live a life of consecration to God and the Church in a spirit of collaboration with the Oblates. They take interest in the activities willed by St. Marello and share in the spiritual benefits, rendering service within or outside the Oblate communities under the direction of the superior.

As associates, they live the spirituality of St. Joseph according to the model of St. Marello, join with the Oblates in prayer, and work closely with the Oblates in service to Christ and the Church.

The commitment to be a Lay Associate includes private consecration with promises to serve God in imitation of St. Joseph (humility, hidden life, hard work, union with Jesus). The preparation of an associate in the Oblates of St. Joseph will include learning to grow spiritually, active ministry and a life of prayer and service.

God's Call

It is the Lord who chooses and calls those whom he desires "… to follow more closely the divine Master" (St. Marello). To help discover His call, men who feel called to join the Oblates of St. Joseph program as a priest or brother are encouraged to prayerfully consider the nature and purpose of their decision.

If you would like more information about the Oblates of St. Joseph, please write to the Oblates of St. Joseph, 544 W. Cliff Dr., Santa Cruz, CA 95060-6147, telephone (831) 457-1868, or send an e-mail to provincial@osjoseph.org. Visit the Oblates of St. Joseph website at www.osjoseph.org.

PRAYER FOR VOCATIONS

O Jesus, the Good Shepherd, when You saw Your people abandoned like sheep without a shepherd you said, "The harvest is rich, but the laborers are scarce," and you urged us to pray to your Heavenly Father to send workers to gather his harvest. Through the intercession of your most Holy Mother Mary, St. Joseph and all the Saints, graciously hear our prayer. Send to your Church many workers filled with zeal for the salvation of souls. Grant our request by the most Precious Blood which you shed for us and by the merits of your Sacred Heart. **Amen.**

JOSEPH: THE MAN CLOSEST TO CHRIST

I f this book has inspired to you learn more about St. Joseph and to become more like him in the many virtues he demonstrates, you will also enjoy the video *Joseph: The Man Closest To Christ*. This 65-minute presentation (available on DVD) features insights and commentary from a variety of Catholic speakers and teachers, and explores all aspects of St. Joseph – the historical man, his response to God's call and the many ways in which he reflects the nature of God.

A companion book to this video presentation – *Tools From Joseph's Workshop: A 30-Day Apprenticeship With The Man Closest To Christ* – is also available. Written by Rick Sarkisian, Ph.D., this 30-day men's devotional demonstrates the "tools" for building Joseph's virtues into your daily life and becoming the authentic man God wants you to be.

Joseph: The Man Closest To Christ and *Tools From Joseph's Workshop* are both part of the LifeWork Press library of life-purpose books and videos by Rick Sarkisian, Ph.D. Ask for a complete product brochure when you order!

To order, call Ignatius Press
toll-free (800) 651-1531 or visit www.ignatius.com